The First New Testament

by
DAVID ESTRADA
and
WILLIAM WHITE, JR.

THOMAS NELSON INC., PUBLISHERS
Nashville • New York

Bible quotations are the authors' translations.

Copyright © 1978 by Thomas Nelson Inc.

Library of Congress Cataloging in Publication Data

Estrada, David.
    The first New Testament.

    Bibliography: p. 141
    1. Dead Sea scrolls—Criticism, interpretation,
etc.   2. O'Callaghan, José.   3. Qumran.   4. Bible.
N. T.—Manuscripts, Greek.   I. White, William,
1934–   joint author.   II. Title.
BM487.E84   225.4'8   78–4057
ISBN 0–8407–5121–4

Contents

Acknowledgments

THE AUTHORS and publisher wish to thank Dr. John Skilton for his interest and inspiration in the writing of this book and Mr. Robert Coote, former managing editor of *Eternity*, for his untiring efforts and invaluable observations on the fragments. Many of his insights are incorporated in this book; also Mr. William White, III, for many of the photographs taken in Israel and Italy; also Mr. David Rubinger, one of the foremost photographers in the Middle East, for his magnificent photographs of the fragments from Cave 7 at Qumran; also Ms. Julia S. Hough for accurate translation of the French notes in the *editio princeps*.

In addition, mention must be made of the cooperation of the Rockefeller Museum, in Jerusalem, Israel; the Biblioteca Apostolica, in the Stato Della Citta Del Vaticano, Rome, Italy; John Rylands University Library, Manchester, England; Oxford University Press, Oxford, England; Houghton Library, Harvard University, Cambridge, Massachusetts; and the Library of the Westminster Theological Seminary, Philadelphia, Pennsylvania.

Illustrations

Introduction

MY PROPOSITION that purports to identify Fragment 5 from Qumran Cave 7 with Mark 6:52,53 has been around now for several years. Sufficient time has been given to anticipate any possible scientific refutation of my New Testament hypothesis.

The authors of the present book know that for at least four years I have been considering the publication of a similar work. But they can also give testimony to the fact that I have resisted the idea for the simple reason that I felt it best to wait longer. I wanted to see if any of my colleagues could propose some literary context in which the material found in Fragment 5 would be better accommodated. By the time this work goes to press, it will have been six years from the appearance of the first article in which I proposed my hypothesis "for the consideration of my colleagues worldwide. And they will pass on whether the identifications are acceptable."[1]

Since then the articles for and against my proposition have been innumerable. As Wilbur N. Pickering says quite correctly, my hypothesis "produced a flurry of reaction. The implications of such an identification are such that I suppose it

---

[1] "New Testament Papyri in Qumran Cave 7?", *Biblica*, 53, 1972, p. 93.

was inevitable that much of the reaction should be partisan."[2] This could perhaps explain the excessive radicality of some refutations, which while apparently supported by an abundance of stated reasons, nevertheless are lacking in any convincing scientific explanations. In the field of scientific discussion, theories cannot be rejected just because the person opposing them does not care to have them accepted. The theory must be allowed to stand unless convincing, rigorous arguments can be brought forward to annul the proposed hypothesis at the scientific level. But I believe that in the case with which we are presently concerned no refutation has been presented that has achieved this goal. Although it would be proper to repeat here what I have written elsewhere, I will say again that I do not have much respect for a colleague—whose competence in the area of New Testament research is undeniable—who has devoted several hours of his labors to refuting my theory. Nevertheless, "he has not been able thus far to handle the one argument that would be the decisive factor for papyrologists in rejecting my theory: to come up with an identification of 7Q5 [Cave 7, Qumran, Fragment 5] that totally rejects the Mark identification."[3]

This is what in large part has motivated me at present to accept the task of writing these brief lines of introduction to the work that the authors have so carefully prepared. I would like to point out here that initially my work centered exclusively around the identification of 7Q5. My colleague, Prof. B. Llorca, has quite correctly noted in the edition of my work on the 7Q papyri: "We have evidence that O'Callaghan has worked only with 7Q5, but at the instigation of other colleagues who helped him in formulating his hypothesis, he has proceeded to investigate whether other fragments of 7Q

---

[2] Wilbur N. Pickering, *The Identity of the New Testament Text* (Nashville: Thomas Nelson, 1977) p. 145.

[3] 7Q5: Some New Considerations", *Studia Papyrologica*, 16, 1977, p. 47, n. 11,3.

might contain New Testament pericopes, since it is quite rare for just one New Testament papyrus, that of Mark, to be found in that particular cave. This was the motivation behind the other specific studies: to check whether 7Q might contain other New Testament texts. But, with the exception of 7Q4, concerning which it may be rejected that it belongs to the Septuagint, O'Callaghan's position with regard to the smaller fragments was only that of recognizing a possible attribution to the New Testament."[4]

Taking these words into account, it could be unquestionably affirmed that not a few of the authors who have fought against my theory never took into account my initial position and mercilessly attacked the smaller passages, seeing in them some other Old Testament attributions, thus discrediting the identification I have proposed. Here I would merely recall that individualizations of the smaller fragments have involved very little effort and time on my part, as the authors of the present work have noted: "Within a few more hours of checking other New Testament texts, O'Callaghan was able to identify eight more of the Cave 7 fragments." In view of the diminutive size of these fragments—and here I quote words written sometime ago—"I do not regard it as necessary to supply the proof required [that is, determine whether they belong to the Septuagint], since it is evident that the smaller the number of letters in a papyrus, the greater the possibility of textual attribution. Furthermore, I do not believe it is necessary to add that my theory was based on the less significant fragments of 7Q, the fact that they exclusively belong to the New Testament having been regarded as uncertain from the very beginning."[5] And these are precisely the fragments that have been most seriously attacked.

---

[4]*Studia Papyrologica*, 13, 1974, p. 130.
[5]*The Greek Papyri of Qumran Cave 7*, Biblioteca de Autores Cristianos 353, Madrid, 1974, p. 89, n. 2.

Because there are several other objections to my identification of Fragment 5, I wish to call attention to some ideas, really quite elemental, of paleographic science. It seems quite incredible that a case should be argued while omitting certain basic principles of paleography, but this is the way the refutations have actually been formulated. Let us recall these concepts:

> It is also worth calling attention to the basic concept that an incomplete and uncertain letter is not the same as an incomplete and certain letter. The latter is as useful in identification as letters that are completely visible . . . we should also keep in mind that the incomplete and uncertain letters can be useful in a negative way for identification, insofar as their remains are incompatible with the shape of the other letters required in an attempt to establish a literary text.[6]

As it is already a matter of public knowledge that the computer is checking the possibility of finding some literary text that better fits the content of 7Q5, and in view of certain articles that have been written on its results, I would like to stress once more that "one and the same manuscript never presents the possibility of a double disposition of the letters. Consequently much computer data can be automatically discounted and confronted with the arrangement of the letters of the original manuscript."[7]

Furthermore, I feel that it would be good to point out that during the entire formulation of my theory I never claimed it as a work of apologetics. It is obvious that when one is operating at the level of pure science, any apologetic claim is at best inadmissable. My hypothesis is purely a matter of identification. And I can now come forward with two other identifications, in which, as before, I have made no pretense at apologet-

---

[6]"The Identifications of 7Q", *Aegyptus*, 56, 1976, p. 289–290.
[7]"The Identifications of 7Q", p. 290.

ics. These are the works of Eusebius of Caesarea, *Historia Ecclesiastica*, Romans 6:43,7–8,11–12 (in PBerl., inv. 17076) and that of Theocritus, I, 31–35, 73–78 (in PBerl., inv. 17073). To pursue apologetic purposes in papyrological labors is to be ignorant of the very essence of our scientific task. Apologetic claims go beyond the limits of our specialization.

I wish to end this brief introduction with the same words in which Wilbur N. Pickering concluded his study on the identifications: "Once 7Q5 is firmly identified with Mark 6:52,53, then the probability that 7Q4 is to be identified with 1 Tim. 3:16, 4:1,3 and 7Q8 with James 1:23,24 becomes very strong. The remaining fragments are so small that dogmatism is untenable—O'Callaghan's identifications are possible, but cannot be insisted upon."[8] I would like to say this is a very objective position and correctly summarizes the entire process by which my theory was formulated.

In a manner similar to that pursued in the prologue to my book on the 7Q papyri, I would now like to repeat, from the perspective of six years of efforts and interpretation, that I appreciate the valuable cooperation of all those who have been involved in my labors. Especially those who were involved in the positive aspects of this period and, to no lesser degree, those who gave consideration to the apparently more vulnerable points. All of these have unquestionably contributed effectively to shedding light on a question where the commitment of many people was necessary to clarify the tentative proposition of a single person.

Accordingly, I would like to end these introductory lines by sincerely thanking Dr. David Estrada and Dr. William White, Jr., for the attention they gave to my theory and the conscientious study this entailed. I also wish to acknowledge those the authors have mentioned at the beginning of the work—all those who cooperated with genuine interest and

[8]*The Identity of the New Testament Text*, p. 148.

kind assistance in achieving this goal. Finally, thanks goes to the publishers, Thomas Nelson, for the care with which they brought the present work to its completion.

José O'Callaghan, S.J.

January 1978

1
Startling News From Qumran

IT WAS late autumn 1971 and Christmas was only a few weeks away. The snow and cold lay far to the north, and sunny Barcelona prepared for the greatest festival of the year. Deaf to the holiday throngs and festivities, a gray-haired, middle-aged priest pored over his treasure of ancient books.

He was a man who had spent his entire life studying the distant past. While modern Spain passed through all of the violent episodes of the twentieth century, he had concentrated on the study of ancient languages—Hebrew, Greek, and Latin.

The crowds in the streets outside his study were busy with shopping in preparation for the holidays. But José O'Callaghan was busy preparing a catalog of ancient fragments of the Greek version of the Old Testament. He traced one tiny piece of papyrus after another through the massive books by noted archaeologists.

For many years O'Callaghan had traveled throughout Europe, Israel, and Egypt seeking the timeworn documents from the early days of Christianity. His efforts had been rewarded; he had been appointed to the faculty of the Pontifical Biblical Institute in Rome with its proximity to the

Vatican Library—which holds the greatest collection of early biblical manuscripts in the world.

One day while routinely going through the publications of hundreds of ancient fragments, he turned to the third volume of *Discoveries in the Judaean Desert of Jordan*.[1] As he studied this volume, O'Callaghan came upon the discussion of the fragments of an Exodus passage found in Cave 7 at Qumran. He looked at the pictures of the Exodus fragments and then became intrigued by another caption on the same page: "Fragments not identified." He then caught site of fragment 5 (see Plate II). His eye fell on the combination of Greek letters **NNHC**[2] and he noted the editor's comment that this was probably the common Greek verbal form **ЄΓЄNNHCЄN**, meaning "to beget" or "be father of." (The root of this word appears in our English words "generate" and "generation.") The word appears very frequently in the genealogical passages of the Old Testament; for example, Genesis 4:18: "To Enoch was born Irad and Irad was the father of Mehujael." The phrase "was the father of" is the Greek EGENNĒSEN. Since **NNHC** is not a particularly common combination in the regular Greek vocabulary, this suggestion of the editors seemed promising.

But O'Callaghan searched through his Greek Old Testament in vain. No doubt he simply retraced the futile steps of the *Discoveries'* editors themselves when they had tried to identify the fragment a decade earlier.

As he checked each passage that contained the word EGENNĒSEN, he looked for the key letters on the fragment

---

[1]M. Baillet et al., eds., *Les Petites Grottes De Qumran*, 2 Pts., Vol. 3, *Discoveries in the Judaean Desert of Jordan* (London: Oxford University Press, 1962). *Discoveries* is a five volume set containing photos of and technical information about the Dead Sea Scrolls fragments.
[2]The Greek letters in this book are either written as uncial Greek so that comparison with the fragments can be made easily or are transliterated into their English equivalents.

that proceeded and followed **NNHC**. For the third line of the fragment O'Callaghan needed to find a **KAI**, the Greek word for "And"; for the second line he needed to find the letter combination " **TN**"; and for the fifth line he needed the Greek letter "eta," " **H**." Since the identifications of fragments 1 and 2 revealed that the original texts ran from sixteen to twenty-three letters per line, O'Callaghan hazarded the guess that fragment 5 might be comparable. If he could match it with a biblical passage and maintain about twenty letters or so per line, he would have an important bit of confirming evidence.

But every Old Testament passage O'Callaghan checked simply did not meet these requirements. Even the easiest word to find, **KAI**, usually appeared too near or too far from the **NNHC**; or there was no logical reason for the space before the **KAI** as it appears on fragment 5. And of course, there was the difficulty of finding the proper letters in the second and fifth lines.

O'Callaghan had classes to teach, administrative reponsibilities to fulfill, and books to complete, and so he put the matter aside. But from time to time he returned to the fascinating question of fragment 5. However, he kept going back over in his mind the odd combination—**NNHC** and the free-standing **KAI** only one line above.

Gennesaret

As O'Callaghan tells it, one evening a few days before Christmas as he relaxed after a busy day, his mind ranged over the day's activities and he thought again of the tiny fragment and the **NNHC**. Suddenly, as if from heaven itself, a new word came to him—not the Old Testament EGENNĒSEN but the familiar place name GENNĒSARET. But as soon as the thought struck him he realized that this was impossible. *Gennesaret* is especially a *New* Testament word. How could

15

Plate I
Father José O'Callaghan

fragment 5, by any stretch of the imagination, be from the New Testament? No, he told himself, it was impossible, absolutely impossible. The tiny scrap had been dated between 50 B.C. and A.D. 50; it could not possibly correspond to something from the New Testament. After all, Qumran is famous for its *Old* Testament finds! And as much as some scholars have wanted to prove otherwise, there seems to be no particular link between the early followers of Christ and the Essene community that lived and worked at this ancient desert retreat called Qumran. No Christian literature whatsoever had ever turned up in these caves. Furthermore, there was no archaeological evidence that Christians had ever used the Qumran caves.

Nevertheless, O'Callaghan left his Old Testament search and turned to his Greek New Testament. *Gennesaret* is an Aramaic place name brought into the vocabulary of the early Greek-speaking Christians because of its role in the ministry of Christ. It appears once each in the Gospels of Matthew, Mark, and Luke. The Luke occurrence, 5:1, is in connection with Jesus' teaching on the shore of Lake Gennesaret, commonly called the Sea of Galilee. In the Matthew and Mark passages, 14:34 and 6:53 respectively, the context is the scene of the feeding of the five thousand and Christ's subsequent return to the village of Gennesaret on the northwest shore of the Sea of Galilee. The Matthew and Mark passages are almost exact parallels.

O'Callaghan must have been excited by the Matthew text, for a **KΔI** appears approximately the right distance before the **NNHC** of *Gennesaret*, and the two letters appear as needed in the line above **KΔI**. But O'Callaghan still had to locate the letter "eta" for the last line of the fragment. There was none in the Matthew account.

He knew it was phenomenal to have come that close to matching the four lines, so he turned quickly to Mark 6:53. His anticipation soared as he laid out the lines to the

Plate II
Fragment 5 from Qumran Cave 7

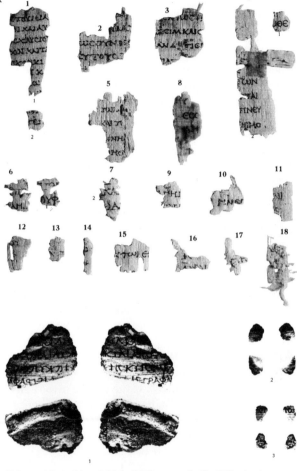

7Q: Papyrus. **1.** Exode. **2.** Lettre de Jérémie. **3–18.** Fragments non identifiés. **19.** Empreintes de papyrus

Plate III

This is Plate XXX from *Discoveries in the Judaean Desert, III*. Notice that fragments 3–18 are listed as "not identified." The reproductions at the top of the plate were enhanced by using the original photograph used by Oxford University Press. (Used by permission of Oxford University Press, Oxford, England.)

approximate measure of twenty characters to the line. This length is used in fragment 1 and appears frequently on other uncial papyri. This time an "eta" appeared just as required in the last line! Furthermore, all the other letters on the fragment could be reconciled to the passage, including the tiny trace of an epsilon, a short "e," on the first line.

In O'Callaghan's own words, "Everything fitted perfectly; 7Q5 [cave 7, Qumran, fragment 5] corresponded to Mark 6:52,53. As a papyrologist the identification was evident. Nevertheless, I couldn't believe it: I thought that everything was the product of my fantasy. Perhaps I was too tired and exhausted. For four days I put the matter aside, and on the fifth day I went back to the manuscript and checked it again. This time, I was convinced."

Equally astounding was the fact that within a few more hours of checking other New Testament texts, O'Callaghan was able to identify eight more of the Cave 7 fragments. If all this was true, then hidden among the minute scraps of the Dead Sea Scrolls was the earliest portion of the New Testament ever found! His comment in the Vatican journal was certainly a scholarly understatement: "I found it very difficult to consider myself in the presence of New Testament papyri, more or less datable to the middle of the first century." Again and again, O'Callaghan kept insisting to himself that the whole idea was impossible. No one had ever dreamed of finding New Testament fragments among the Scrolls. But the evidence could no longer be denied.

The Public Announcement

Although he reached this conclusion about Christmastime 1971, it was not until he had convinced some of his colleagues of its validity that he was prepared to declare his identification in print. He announced his identification in a public talk given in Barcelona in February of 1972. Soon afterward, he went to

Rome to take up his duties at the Pontifical Institute. It was to his advantage that one of his nearby colleagues was Father Carlo M. Martini, Rector of the Pontifical Biblical Institute and a New Testament scholar of the first rank. In fact, Father Martini was one of the five scholars who prepared the second edition of the Greek New Testament published by the United Bible Societies in 1968.

No more difficult or expert audience could have been found than the professors of the Institute. In many hours of discussion and explanation O'Callaghan was challenged relentlessly at every critical point. Finally however, the sheer weight of the evidence convinced his colleagues, and for them also the impossible became possible—and probable.

Finally convinced himself, Father Martini provided an article of his own that appeared with O'Callaghan's first publication on his find. It appeared in March 1972, in the fifty-third volume, first fascicle, of *Biblica*, (in Spanish the article was entitled "Papiros neotestamentarios en la cueva 7 de Qumran?"). The Society of Biblical Literature provided its members with an English translation of both articles as a supplement to the *Journal of Biblical Literature* (Vol. 91, No. 2, 1972). But even though the article was couched in careful academic terms and meticulously covered the evidence, its ten pages and eighteen footnotes in five languages struck the sedate world of New Testament scholarship like a tidal wave.

2
The Find of the Century

O N MARCH 18, 1972, news media around the world carried the story that a fragment of the Gospel of Mark had been found among the Dead Sea Scrolls. The identification, made by a Spanish-Catalan Jesuit scholar, Father José O'Callaghan of Barcelona, Spain, was made public by him in a talk in that city.

Newspapers across the United States picked up the story. The essentials of O'Callaghan's proposed identification were distributed by the international wire services and quickly appeared around the world in more than one hundred languages.

The New York Times reported:

"If Father O'Callaghan's theory is accepted it would prove that at least one of the gospels—that of St. Mark—was written only a few years after the death of Jesus."

The *Chicago Tribune* stated:

"If this theory is accepted by scholars, biblical research would be revolutionized."

The *Los Angeles Times* wrote:

"Nine New Testament fragments, dated A.D. 50 to A.D. 100, have been discovered in a Dead Sea cave and if validated, constitute the most sensational Biblical trove uncovered in recent times."

However, for most interested readers in the English-speaking world, the first detailed presentation they saw of O'Callaghan's proposal was in the June 1972 issue of the popular religious monthly *Eternity*. The then managing editor, Robert Coote, whose work and observations are so much a part of this book, organized three articles covering O'Callaghan's work and identifications of the fragments from Cave 7.

The first article, entitled "The Fragments from Cave 7," was an interview with Father O'Callaghan by David Estrada; the second, "A Layman's Guide to O'Callaghan's Discovery," was written by William White, Jr.; and the third article was entitled "On Dating the New Testament" by F. F. Bruce.

The immediate reaction was a distinct "numb." It seemed for a number of months that the entire "establishment" of biblical scholarship had been caught without any prior expectation that a first-century portion from the New Testament would ever be found. A quick criticism of O'Callaghan was difficult because he had neither found nor dated the fragments. Thus, there was no reason to dispute the date. In fact, he had not even deciphered the letters—the editors of *Discoveries* had done that a decade earlier—however, O'Callaghan did propose major alterations in the reading of some indistinct letters.

The mood of quiet did not last long. By the fall of 1972 an enormous storm of protest had broken out over the tiny fragments from Cave 7. The storm of dissent and the heat of criticism came on like the sudden showers over the desert that turn the dry wadis into raging torrents. Unlike the initial announcement of the finding of the Dead Sea Scrolls in 1948, which took years to reach the hearts and convictions of scholars, the announcement of March 1972 was taken seriously from the first day.

The reactions ranged from open approval through admonitions of caution, to outright rejection:

> We must, of course, await further developments. But we await with a decided sense of eagerness; for such evidence would not only clear the field of many useless speculations, but also serve as a catalyst for important and constructive investigation of the New Testament.[1]

> Richard N. Longenecker
> Trinity Evangelical Divinity School

> The new fragments open up large new fields of investigations. An intriguing prospect is that scholars may find more such remarkable items now that Dr. O'Callaghan has shown us where to look[2]

> R. Laird Harris
> Covenant Theological Seminary

> The most that can be said with any degree of confidence, it seems to me, is that these three fragments appear to be from very ancient copies of Mark and James.[3]

> Bruce M. Metzger
> Princeton Theological Seminary

> I would say that the identity of the fragments is still not certain. More thorough examination of the originals themselves is

[1]*Eternity*, July 1972.
[2]*Ibid.*
[3]*Eternity*, June 1972.

needed. Since the amount of evidence is so slender, any certainty about the identity of these fragments will have to come to rest upon expert analysis of all possible alternative identifications with known documents of this period. I am hopeful but not convinced at this point.[4]

Alan F. Johnson
Wheaton College

It would be exciting and welcome news indeed if his (O'Callaghan's) suggestions would be substantiated, but they must be regarded thus far as being *sub judice*.[5]

F. F. Bruce
University of Manchester

O'Callaghan's identification is perhaps possible; it seems to me to be most highly improbable. In any case, the "find" can never be used with certainty and the discussion as to the date of Mark's Gospel is very much where it was before O'Callaghan's discovery.[6]

Gordon D. Fee
Wheaton College

Clearly, in every field of research, intuition and speculation are legitimate, and even fun. But it is advisable not to draw conclusions from them until they are backed by facts.[7]

G. Ernest Wright
Harvard University

---

[4]*Eternity*, July, 1972
[5]"O'Callaghan's Fragments: Our Earliest New Testament Texts," *The Evangelical Quarterly*, Vol. 45, No. 1, Jan.–Mar. 1973.
[6]"Some Dissenting Notes on 7Q5=Mark 6:52,53," *Journal of Biblical Literature*, Dec. 1972.
[7]"Are New Testament Manuscripts to be Found Among the Dead Sea Scrolls?" *American Schools of Oriental Research News Letter*, No. 11, June 1972.

Identifications on this scale are an exercise not in scholarship but in fantasy.[8]

C. H. Roberts
Discoveries consultant

The very fact that so many distinguished scholars so immediately presented such a wide diversity of opinion is of prime importance. Why should the world of biblical scholarship—both conservative and liberal—take such awesome offense at the possible discovery of the oldest fragments of the New Testament ever found? Why was O'Callaghan greeted with jeers and acidic criticism instead of an immediate effort to locate more first-century material?

The answer to these two questions points out the tremendous importance of O'Callaghan's identifications and the serious challenge it presents to the basic view of Scripture held by many modern theologians and biblical scholars, a view that has cast doubt on the authenticity and historicity of the New Testament. To answer these questions, however, we will have to review the history of the study of the New Testament text, and we will have to understand the positions taken by contemporary scholars regarding the New Testament.

The New Testament Text

The New Testament was written in Greek and passed on by means of handwritten copies up until the Renaissance. After the invention of the printing press in the fourteenth century, the Latin Vulgate Bible was published, but it took another century and a half before a Greek text was finally printed in 1516. This edition, originally made by the Dutch scholar Erasmus of Rotterdam, became the commonly accepted

[8]Letter to the London *Times*, April 7, 1972.

27

Greek text and in 1633 became known as the *textus receptus* or "received text." However, as more and older manuscripts were discovered, there was a continual editing of the Greek text to reflect the readings of these older manuscripts.

The process of editing continued, and in 1831 Charles Lachmann produced the first edition of the Greek New Testament that completely ignored the readings of the *textus receptus*. He was attempting to publish the text of the New Testament as it was in A.D. 350.

During the 1800s, the German nobleman Lobegott Friedrich Konstantin von Tischendorf became the most important scholar seeking to support the authority of the New Testament and the accuracy of the picture it gives of the divine incarnation of Jesus Christ into human history. Tischendorf, a very pious Lutheran, was deeply upset at the rather slovenly way arguments against the authority and historical accuracy of the New Testament were carried on.

It is said that Tischendorf had as his motto, "Jesus Christ called Himself the Truth and not the Habit," meaning that tradition alone was not sufficient for understanding the Scriptures, but that creative scholarship was needed to fight the scholarship of those critical of the Bible. And so he set out to survey and compare the available manuscripts in virtually all the museums of Europe and to search for new manuscripts in the Middle East.

Tischendorf's greatest find was discovered in the ancient bone-littered library of the Monastery of St. Catherine, perched high on Mount Sinai in the center of the desert between Israel and Arabia. There he discovered a very early uncial codex (a codex is a manuscript in *book* form, not in scroll form). It was dated to within three hundred and fifty years after the birth of Jesus Christ. Because of the discovery site, it was named *Codex Sinaiticus* (see Plate IV).

For a number of centuries, there had existed a great uncial codex in the Vatican Library in Rome called the *Vaticanus*

ΤΗΕΡΙΙΜШ·ΕΥΟΥ
ΝΑΤΕΓΙΙΝΟΛΟΝΚῩ
ΚΛΟШΣΕΙΙΕΝΗ·Α
ΙΛϹΟΙΙΡΟΦΙΓΙΙΙϹ:

Plate IV
Example of the style of writing in the Codex Sinaiticus

ΤΟΥΛΛΛΟΥΝΤΟΣΚΑΙΗ
ΝΟΛΟΥΘΗΣΑΝΤШΙΥϹΤΥ
ΦΕΙϹΛΕΟΙΟΚΛΙΘΕΛϹΑ
ΜΕΝΟϹΑΥΤΟΥϹΛΚΟ

Plate V
Example of the style of writing in the Codex Vaticanus

(see Plate V). The *Vaticanus* became known to the textual scholars by the abbreviation capital "B," and the new *Sinaiticus* became known as "Aleph," the first letter of the Hebrew alphabet. These two, written sometime in the fourth century A.D., were book-type, that is, with pages bound on the left margin, and were written in magnificent capital-letter Greek.

These codices became the basis for most of the critical editions of the New Testament. Very careful study of the two great uncial codices proved that they were indeed earlier and better preserved than many of the other manuscripts that had been available to Erasmus and his immediate followers.

Tischendorf's find, which first went to the royal Russian Library of the Czar and finally to the British Museum, was one of the greatest manuscript discoveries of the nineteenth century. However, Tischendorf continued to try to produce a Greek New Testament which would pick and choose among the manuscripts according to their relative qualities and strengths to finally produce the most authoritative Greek text. The great debate, however, hinged upon just how the texts and their readings were to be chosen.

Westcott and Hort

In 1872, Tischendorf completed his massive edition of the Greek New Testament, one of the most complete and detailed ever published. However, only nine years later two English scholars, Brooke Foss Westcott and Fenton John Anthony Hort, published a critical edition of the Greek New Testament with an introductory volume actually longer than the entire New Testament text. Almost within the year of its publication, the Westcott and Hort edition became the most widely received and used of all of the many critical editions.

Largely utilizing the readings or traditions of the two great uncial codices, *Sinaiticus* and *Vaticanus*, Westcott and Hort totally rejected the readings or traditions of the miniscule manuscripts. They studied virtually no papyri or sources earlier than the fourth-century codices. In fact, in their extensive introduction, they did not mention the papyri even once.

Westcott and Hort made many assumptions about the relative value and authenticity of the uncial and miniscule manuscripts in their possession. (Uncial manuscripts are written in what might be compared to capital printed letters, having been developed from carving in stone, and are older than miniscule manuscripts which are written in what might be compared to script writing.) One of Westcott and Hort's least scientific conclusions was that the earliest New Testament would have the shortest and most simple but elegant readings. However, this and other of their assumptions have proven defective as earlier texts have been discovered.

Vaticanus and *Sinaiticus* were discovered in the nineteenth century. Since they were earlier and much more elegant than the mass of codices in miniscule writing, they were given greater weight in decisions about the readings of the text. But in the twentieth century, uncial codices made from leaves of papyrus bound as books began to appear. While it was suspected by some scholars that an even earlier form had existed—that is, earlier uncials written on papyrus scrolls—no physical remains of them had been found.

The continual recovery of earlier and earlier materials added more variant readings, that is, slightly different forms of grammar, at given points in the biblical text. Most of these were nothing more than different spellings of words or slightly different grammatical forms of the words already found in the text. The critical editions, which seemed to blossom almost yearly, were based upon the recovery of these newer papyri and were thereby billed as being more like the original New Testament writings.

It is not in the province of this short narrative of the discoveries at Qumran Cave 7 to go into all of the massive information necessary to present properly the elaborate philosophies that led each individual critic to produce his edition of the Greek text of the New Testament. However, a very fine introduction to the whole history can be found in *The Identity of the New Testament Text* by Wilbur N. Pickering.

The important thing to note is that after the work of Tischendorf and his phenomenal discovery of the *Sinaiticus*, the rush was on to recover more and older New Testament fragments. Strangely enough, however, while many new textual finds were made, particularly in the trash heaps of Egypt dating from the Roman Age, these discoveries did not really influence the view held by scholars in Europe, and later in America, of the origin and formation of the New Testament.

The Quest for the Historical Jesus

It is important to understand the basic ideas of the view held by many nineteenth- and twentieth-century scholars of the origin and formation of the New Testament. There was a laudable effort to recover an earlier and purer New Testament text. At the same time, however, there was a parallel effort to recover a Christianity more pristine and less supernatural than that which had been held for centuries. As early as 1600, there were scholars in England and Germany who questioned the miracles and other supernatural elements in the Bible.

Slowly, over the subsequent one hundred and fifty years, these views became dominant in the university circles of Germany. Many scholars set out on what became known as the "quest for the historical Jesus." This was an attempt to strip away from the New Testament those elements that were thought to be either theological or mythological additions in an attempt to find what was felt to be the true human Jesus of history.

The difficulty is obvious: The diety of Jesus Christ and His *sp.* miracles are such an integral and interwoven part of the Gospel narratives that the only possible way to strip off any purported interpretations that they might bear is to cut out pieces. And so the cutting out of pieces of the text went along with the cutting out of pieces of the theological teaching of the text. This process has gone on into modern times.

This view of Scripture, which sought to strip away the supernatural, was supported by "higher criticism," which started in the early eighteenth century. There are two kinds of criticism of a text. (Criticism here does not mean a review or evaluation, but a close and scientific study.) *Lower criticism* is the scrutiny of the spelling, grammar, vocabulary, and linguistics of the text. *Higher Criticism*, on the other hand, is the more abstract study of the philosophy, history, and interpretation of a text. Positive, Bible-honoring lower and higher criticism does take place but is not well known; negative, Bible-destroying lower and higher criticism has attracted many participants and thus has dominated the field.

The growth of negative higher criticism has been checked at numerous points in its nearly two-hundred-year development by the appearance of discoveries made in linguistics and archaeology. In almost every case, such discoveries have given credence if not authentication to the historical and factual statements of Scripture. However, in the face of negative views of the Bible, which first gained popularity in Germany and later in England, many were swept by the majority opinion into following along. It seems that a theological position once constructed with all of its elegance and beauty is not to be demolished and rebuilt merely because new evidence comes to light. But it is this new archaeological evidence that we *must* take into account.

Archaeological Evidence

The first one to prove that ancient manuscripts could be discovered was the founder of scientific archaeology in Egypt, Flinders Petrie. A typical Victorian dynamo of a man, he was able to excavate many lesser-known sites in Egypt and to fill in gaps in almost every age of Egyptian history. His work was monumental and fundamental since he had to set new standards for accuracy and for careful recording of his finds, including even the most obscure artifacts. Petrie was given permission by the Egyptian government to excavate in the area of the Fayum, an unlikely area of Egypt, where once there had been a vast lake along which was a very extensive series of Greek-period villages.

In the garbage dumps and rather crude graves of these ancient towns he discovered a mass of papyrus scraps containing longer and shorter fragments of many classical Greek works, some of which had been totally lost to scholars since antiquity. His work was followed up by a series of younger scholars—British, German, and American—who succeeded in obtaining many more manuscript finds. It was with this larger effort that the introduction of archaeology came to the forefront as a major factor in dealing with the New Testament and its history.

From the late nineteenth century until the 1920s two English scholars, Bernard Grenfell and Arthur Hunt, did a great deal of rummaging through the trash piles of the ancient Greek towns in Egypt. They took back to England and to the British Museum many, many crates and cartons of papyrus scraps. Needles to say, it took much longer for these to be edited and studied than it did for them to be discovered; therefore, much of the material was not immediately deciphered. However, with the finds of the Grenfell and Hunt expeditions, Greek papyrology could be set on a scientific basis. Enough material was available to trace rather minutely and almost year by year the styles of and changes in handwriting that took place.

Several Germans, chiefly Schubart and von Gardthausen, made exhaustive studies of the changes in paleography (the development of styles of writing). Another German, Adolph Deissmann, studied the nonliterary papyri—shopping lists, children's school papers, and snatches of personal letters. From these Deissmann was able to show the full vocabulary of Koiné Greek[9] and discover numerous parallels with the language of the New Testament. It was on the basis of this painstaking research that the science of papyrology was placed on a firm footing.

The Theory of Oral Tradition

By 1950, most papyri could be dated from internal evidence fairly accurately and precisely. However, the work of the scientific papyrologists did not immediately impress nor reorganize the theories of the critical scholars who were looking for the "historical Jesus." Particularly in Germany, the mythological interpretation of New Testament history that assumed that there had been a long period of oral tradition and a series of rewritings of the material continued in vogue many, many years after the papyri were edited and published.

One of the chief off-beat theories of this type was that Jesus was a teacher, a man of wisdom, almost a popular object of folklore, and that his life and teachings had been theologized first by the apostle Paul and subsequently by others who followed him. This led to the thesis that in effect the Christian church was a creation of the second or even third century and that the earliest life of Jesus, which would be little more than a discontinuous collection of sayings, is unknown.

[9]The common language of Greek-speaking people of the Roman period.

Proponents of these ideas generally assumed that the Gospels of Matthew, Mark, and Luke were somehow related, but that the Gospel of John came from some other source. Certain scholars assumed that the Gospel of Mark was the earliest, others assumed that the Gospel of Matthew was the earliest, and there were many partial theories attributing pieces or segments of one or another Gospel to an earlier written source, which was labeled the "Q" document.

But the basic ingredient of all these theories, the thing that made them possible and the thing that made them work, was *time*! A period of time, it was said, had to have come between the life and teachings of Jesus Himself and the necessary theologizing and mythologizing that came afterward.

Form Criticism

By the 1930s, the weight of papyri discoveries was so great that the critical theory of the reconstruction of the history of the New Testament, which had dominated pre-World War I theological discussions, began to collapse. In its place came a variety of critical theories based upon the comparison of the forms of literature within the New Testament. This is what is known in German as *Formgeschichte* or "form criticism." Form criticism gained a great many adherents primarily through its chief spokesman in the New Testament realm, Rudolph Bultmann. As more and more papyri were discovered, a rather substantial collection of pre-third-century material came to light.

In 1935 the British scholar C. H. Roberts (the same scholar who dated fragment 5 from Qumran 7 in the *Discoveries* volume) published a tiny fragment containing two sections from the Gospel of John: John 18:31–33 was on one side of the fragment and John 18:37,38 was on the other (see Plate XXI). It was found in the John Rylands Library in Manchester, England, and was called Papyrus 52. Roberts, one of the greatest papyrologists of this century, dated the fragment no later than A.D. 135. Since the tradition was that John was the last Gospel written and probably was not written until the very end of the first century, this would put the fragment to within thirty to forty years of the earliest possible writing of that Gospel. The fragment appears to originally have been excavated by Grenfell and Hunt from one of the Roman-period towns in the Egyptian Fayum. Since then other similar papyri have been discovered.

In 1956 the Swiss library Bibliotheca Bodmeriana published a series of papyri of New Testament passages dated between A.D. 150 and 250. But the conception continued that the earliest Christian documents were written by unknown persons on the spur of the moment and in the codex form.

The general view was well stated by C. C. McCowan of the Pacific School of Religion who wrote in 1943,

> Some businessman or housewife may have made the first records of Jesus' words along with business or household accounts. Out of such jottings in Aramaic and Greek some earlier "Matthew" or "Luke" may have compiled the "Sayings of Jesus" which were used in the teaching sections of the first and third Gospels.[10]

This statement summarizes the general opinion of the majority of New Testament scholars to this day, and it is doubtful that even tons of papyri would shake their belief. After all, it took nearly three centuries for German negative higher criticism to win the day and become the dominant opinion in academic circles. It is not going to disappear overnight regardless of the evidence that comes forth.

Such doubts about the authenticity and historicity of the

[10]"The Earliest Christian Books," *The Biblical Archaeologist*, Vol. 2, May 1943.

New Testament often find their way into popular books on the Bible and widely disseminated Sunday school materials. One example is the *Interpreter's Bible*, which states concerning the Gospel of Mark:

> . . . to all intents and purposes, we must study the Gospel as if it were anonymous, like most of the books of the Bible . . . . not a product of personal literary authorship. . . . the book (Mark) cannot have been written by an eyewitness. It is a compendium of church tradition . . . not the personal observations of a participant.[11]

By the end of World War II and with the discovery of the Dead Sea Scrolls, it became evident that a new insight into the text and history of early Christianity would come as a result of archaeology. But despite the general acceptance of this idea, most scholars thoroughly imbued with negative higher critical views continued to ignore both the evidence and its conclusions. They merely proposed newer hypotheses to prove the basic correctness of nineteenth-century theories. There was no radical criticism of the Wescott and Hort hypothesis of the text and no rejection of the idea that the New Testament developed from essentially oral traditions over one or more centuries. But, like it or not, the age of archaeology had come and new understandings of linguistics followed close behind.

The Situation Today

In the early years of the twentieth century the antagonism between conservative evangelicals and more liberal theologians reached a flash point. Many conservatives, such as John Gresham Machen, were forced out of the great

---

[11]*Interpreter's Bible*, Vol. 7 (Nashville: Abingdon, 1947).

denominations and thus became part of a "third force" in the Christian world. This then created three groupings within Christendom—the Roman Catholics, the traditional Protestants, and the new separatist evangelicals.

The events of World War II brought about profound changes in liberal theology and resulted in the rediscovery of Søren Kierkegaard and the development of dialectic theology. The solitary giant of European Christianity was Karl Barth, and the watchword of the hour was ecumenism. The union of one denomination with another went on apace and culminated in the First and Second Vatican Councils. While the trend toward reducing unimportant and irrelevant historical divisions was certainly worthwhile, the blurring of truly profound theological and philosophical differences simply to gain superficial fraternity was most unfortunate. One aspect of this was the development of mediating positions. And so there appeared all manner of hybrid viewpoints—Neo-orthodox, Neo-evangelical, Neo-fundamentalists—and on the other side of the issue, constructive liberalism and cooperative evangelism.

In this climate there also developed an uneasy peace between the traditionally liberal views of Scripture and the more conservative views. The first result of this mixture of eclectic interchange has been a mass confusion: lay people have been left in a quandary not knowing whom to believe. The "genius" of dialectic theology is that it permits the continued use of biblical terms—sin, salvation, atonement, sanctification (to mention only a few)—yet radically reinterprets each one of them so that they no longer present a true biblical theology but instead convey man-made philosophies. Millions of churchgoers continue to believe that the words of Jesus in the New Testament were actually spoken by Him. But the professors in the seminaries apply the twisted logic of the eighteenth-century German philosopher Immanuel Kant and disguise their basic unbelief in the credibility of the New

Testament with their layers of academic but unintelligible jargon.

In the decades of the 1950s and 1960s it was not unusual to find students from fundamentalist backgrounds pursuing doctorates in traditionally liberal institutions. The result of this mutual recognition was a glossing over of the hard facts of the Scriptures' historical claims. While the naive tradition of conservatives would have maintained that the apostles, evangelists, and other authors of the New Testament did indeed directly write or dictate the books ascribed to them, the trend altered this so that both neo-evangelicals and constructive liberals could agree on some sort of period of oral or informal written transmission.

The accommodation of liberal theology by mainline denominations was moving into its second and third generation when O'Callaghan dropped into its midst what has since proved to be an enormous problem and an embarrassment to mediating conservatives as well as liberals. This is why biblical scholars took offense at his discovery and greeted it with jeers and acidic criticism. And, as if the stirring up of these waters was not enough, the identification of the fragments from Cave 7 at Qumran also caused unrelieved tensions in another touchy area, the troubled balance of forces in the state of Israel.

According to an agreement made after the discovery of the Dead Sea Scrolls, there are at least four parties involved in overseeing and researching the find. They are the Department of Antiquities of Israel, the American School of Oriental Research, the Rockefeller Museum, and the École Biblique et Archéologique. After centuries of persecution by misguided Christians, the Israeli authorities are not enthusiastic about any research that centers on the Crucifixion or the early days of Christianity. In fact, many excavated artifacts that the

Israeli government believes might stir up controversy are simply not displayed.

The Israeli experts fought long and hard to establish the authenticity and early date of the Dead Sea Scrolls. However, they would be just as well satisfied if there were no study of this material for purely Christian ends. Into this uneasy balance of forces, O'Callaghan dropped his intellectual bomb. It is no wonder that from every side violent reaction resulted.

One Footprint

The end of this antagonism is not in sight. In fact, the authors of this book withheld their work on the fragments for five years, after being assured by both friend and foe that a completely acceptable interpretation of the fragments would soon be found. The fact is that nearly every great mind in the world of New Testament scholarship has worked overtime to produce such a face-saving and tension relieving interpretation. After five years, many suggestions, dozens of learned papers, and a number of computer trials, no alternative identification has emerged.

This book is the fruition of all the debates and trials. The material from Cave 7 is so small and provides so little text for comparison and examination that no final probability can be assigned. However, as in the classic case of Robinson Crusoe who only needed one footprint to prove the presence of another man, so the simple case of fragment 5 is evidence enough that sooner or later more first-century fragments of the New Testament will indeed be found. In this light, New Testament scholars may as well begin rethinking their stance as to the origins and authenticity of the text. It is our contention and expectation that the tiny scraps from Cave 7 are only the beginning of their woes.

41

3
The Land, the Book, and the People

I N THE opinion of many, the Dead Sea Scrolls constitute the most exciting and controversial discovery affecting biblical studies in this century. To tell the story of these tiny scraps of papyrus found in a hillside cave high above the Dead Sea, we will start in Jerusalem.

We begin the journey to the Dead Sea and the Qumran caves among the busy jostling throngs and the narrow, crowded streets of the ancient city. The main road, which is known as King David Street, winds along until it passes small shops and an incredible scene of humanity: Arabs, Jews, and Christians from Europe and Asia, all in native costumes, represent many nations of the world. Men from Arab villages wear western clothes with the traditional white headdress and braided cord, and Arab women wear black skirts and brightly colored shawls. Here and there is an Arab nomad wearing a flowing robe (called a *burnoose*) tied with a multicolored sash. An occasional older Arab will wear the red-felt *tarbush*, a pot-shaped hat with a tail of black braid. The Israelis wear parts of olive-colored uniforms with summer sport shirts. The streets around the orthodox quarter, called *Me'a Sharim*, are crowded with the Hassidic Jews—the ultraorthodox wearing long black coats and broad-brimmed hats—the reminders of their origins in seventeenth-century Europe.

The whole history of Christianity passes in review. The priests and deacons of ancient African churches and the Syrian- and Greek-rite priests and their disciples all mix and rub shoulders in the same bustling crowds. However, it is the great legion of Roman Catholic clergy and laity that adds color to the incredible panorama. The Franciscans with sandals and cowls, the intensely intellectual Jesuits, and the large numbers of Dominicans and Augustinians all add to the kaleidoscope of liturgy and pious practice—a prayerbook of the ages in human form.

After passing through most of the town and heading south, one comes to the Old City. It was this section of Jerusalem that was divided by barricades and barbed wire from 1948 until it was won by the Israelis in 1967. The devastation and remains of that bitter war are seen all around the Old City: great thick fortifications pockmarked by shell holes and rocket blasts, endless miles of twisted, rusted, concertina wire, and great holes in the earth that have only partially been refilled. Surely Jerusalem is the most fought over city in the world.

Going from the new Eastern city of the Jews to the old Western city of the Arabs, the immediate contrast in physical and social conditions is shocking to anyone. Older buildings with Turkish and Arab names, narrower streets, rusty, dirty-green buses, and an incredible mass of rural humanity with their donkeys suddenly greets one and makes it clear that there are two nations within one. On the right is the wall of the Old City with its many gates and its masses of sellers and buyers and lenders and borrowers passing in and out on their daily round of merchandising. This is the Street of the Paratroopers, named for Israel's heroes; to the left are the remains of the Arab administration, banks, post offices, and long lines of shops. Almost at the very end of the wall, the ground rises, and to the left there is the old Rockefeller Museum. The fragments from Qumran are locked away in the celler of this fortress-like building brooding behind high fences and heavy walls on its solitary hill.

All along the roadside are the remains of the former Jordanian administration. Evidence of those peaceful years abound here and there: Arab names beautifully carved in the high walls and the ornate road signs on their concrete standards. A sharp turn at the end of the Old City wall brings one to the Jericho Road. It was a traveler on this road that Jesus told about in the story of the Good Samaritan.

The road branches off with one way going around the crest of the Mount of Olives. It passes ancient rock-cut tombs dating back to the second century B.C. Other burial grounds, each facing the temple mount, were desecrated and destroyed during the recent wars over this most sacred of all cemeteries. The road again rises up a hill around the Mount of Olives and then the city disappears as the traveler continues on through Arab villages and begins the long descent that will take him down to the shore of the Dead Sea a thousand feet below sea level, the lowest spot on earth. While the Judean hills on the journey from Tel Aviv to Jerusalem are covered with trees and brooks and vegetation of all sorts, the Judean hills along the descent from Jerusalem to Jericho are desolate and barren. Vast masses of gravel and stone stand out on the land, which appears to be totally dry and almost sterile.

The empty vastness is broken here and there by flocks of sheep tended by Arab shepherds. The landscape is dotted with black goat-skin tents in which women, completely clothed in black, cook meals for their families in the same manner as their female ancestors of old. Here and there, camels graze on the stubble grass and flocks of goats surefootedly skip from rock to rock. Roads on each side of the main one show the tracks of heavy Israeli army tanks, and very few hours go by without the scream and vibration of the streaking jet fighter planes that constantly survey the border between Jordan and Israel.

The road continues down and down mile after mile until finally in the distance to the right is the blue-green of the Salt or Dead Sea. In the far distance, on its opposite shore, are the mountains of Jordan set against a rosy-red sky that turns to blue and then to purple as the sun passes over and sets behind them. As the road continues to wind and descend there is a fork to the left leading to the oasis of Jericho, probably the oldest continuously inhabited city in the world. It is visible in the near distance—a bright patch of inviting green amid the endless sand and gravel.

The road to the right takes the traveler down along the shore of the Dead Sea and eventually to the point where the enormous hills and ridges of solid stone and gravel come to within a mile of the seashore itself. It is at one of these ascents, where the mountains are especially close to the seashore, that the pile of ruins called Khirbet Qumran was found. The ruins, not more than several thousand square feet, have been known for centuries, but the archaeologists who first surveyed them assumed they were merely the remains of a Roman military outpost. Such outposts dotted the valley during the Roman era because the Jericho Road was a major trade route to Saudi Arabia and to the East Coast of Africa and consequently was a traditional haunt for robbers. It was in 1947 during the height of the Arab-Israeli war that Khirbet Qumran took on far more important prominence in world history.

The Dead Sea Scrolls

Precisely how or when the Dead Sea Scrolls first came to light cannot now be determined; however, the most popularly repeated story is that an Arab shepherd boy of the nomadic Tamireh tribe, Muhammad Adh-Dhib, was searching for

Plates VI and VII
Along the lifeless, debris-ridden shore of the Dead Sea, rocks and
sand are coated in layers of alkali.

47

some lost goats through the Judean wilderness in February or March of 1947. The story goes that he was throwing stones, as any fifteen-year-old boy might do, when one of them fell into a cave and clunked against a pot. The boy looked in, discovered both pots and scrolls, and either carried off some of the material himself or brought his adult relatives to the spot and they then carried away some of the pots and scrolls. The cave was nearly a mile and a quarter inland from the Dead Sea and situated in the foothills below the higher Judean elevations. Within a mile or so was the old ruin of Khirbet Qumran; the ruin was just south of a line running from the Dead Sea shore to the market town of Bethlehem situated on the far side of the red-rock hills and where on the first Christmas eve, Jesus Christ was born. It was to that town that the first of the scrolls discovered in the pots were taken.

Since the Arabs were on good terms with the Syrian Christian merchants of that area, the next contact was with them. Through these people, the scrolls finally made their way to the Archbishop of the Syrian Orthodox Church at St. Mark's Monastery in the Old City of Jerusalem. Within a few months, the materials had been passed around and seen by a number of antiquities dealers and various members of the archaeological research community in Jerusalem. However, these were times of war and every journey to Qumran was filled with danger; greater issues than antiquities were on the minds of all. But as study of the scrolls went on, a new era in Old Testament understanding began.

What new information did the Qumran scrolls actually bring the world of biblical studies? The first thing they demonstrated was that the text of the Hebrew Bible, which was available in any Jewish bookstore or seminary library throughout the world at that time, was essentially, with some variants, the same Old Testament text that was known in the time of Jesus, and in the case of some books, a century and a half earlier.

Plate VIII
This is the escarpment above Qumran where the small caves were found.

Plate IX
This is one of the large caves discovered across the wadi beneath Qumran.

They also proved that the Jews of antiquity had recognized the authority, supremacy, and extreme importance of this collection of books and had gone to all sorts of efforts to preserve them.

Lastly, they showed that there had been great upheavals and historical developments in Judaism during the Roman era. The scrolls demonstrated that the turmoil within Judaism reported in the New Testament Gospels did indeed take place.

A whole host of Jewish believers in the Old Testament, who were not a part and did not want to be a part of the political and sectarian parties of their time, rejected the elaborate temple administration, which was under Roman control. They also rejected the priests and scribes and the opinions of the Pharisees. They tried to find a simpler, purer form of religion in the Old Testament itself, apart from the traditions and political pressures of the various groups around them. This third force in Jewish history was assumed to be the progenitor, if not the most fertile field, for early Christianity. And in fact, there are many aspects of the Dead Sea Scrolls that are similar to aspects of the New Testament Gospels. The wording and ideas expressed are similar in a number of passages, particularly to some words and phrases in the Gospel of John.

The Land

The discovery of the treasure trove of ancient writings at Qumran is the best known but by no means the only important historical event to take place in the wilderness along the northwest shore of the Dead Sea. This desolate waste has been the scene of many historical events recorded in the Bible and has been the location of world-shaking events right up to the present.

It was along this shore that Abraham sought the land of

God's promise. It was on one of these sand-covered hills that he parted ways with Lot, who traveled south to Sodom and Gomorrah, the cities of the plain. It was along this seashore that he pursued and defeated Chedorlaomer and the confederation of kings. In this ancient trackless waste, Israel wandered in its exodus from Egypt on its way to the "land flowing with milk and honey."

Here the twelve tribes fought with Moab and Midian and the Children of the East. Hundreds of years later, the lad David fled here from Saul, and the prophets and seers of Jehovah often meditated in this austere place. Jesus was tempted by Satan, the accuser, on a mountain a few miles above Jericho overlooking this same Salt Sea. Herod himself built a fortress and retreat some miles south at Masada; across the valley at the fortress of Machaerus, one of his successors had John the Baptist beheaded.

It was to this same lifeless place, with its still and breathless atmosphere and infernal heat, that the seekers after a purer Judaism fled at the beginning of the Roman Age. On a little hill at the foot of the great rocky ridge, they built Qumran and sought in the Holy Scriptures God's final will in history. They spent their lives in holes and caves among these rocks paying homage to their God, brooding over the checkered history of their forefathers, and contemplating the age to come.

The Excavation of Qumran

When peace returned to Israel and Jordan after the 1947 war and archaeological expeditions could be initiated, one of the first places to be excavated was the ruin of Khirbet Qumran. There, a large building was found in which tables and ink wells and other writing paraphenalia were discovered that apparently had been used by a monastic-type sect of Jews who made copying manuscripts their vocation. It appeared that these were probably the writers of the Dead Sea Scrolls.

The problem is that there is no actual physical connection nor evidence directly linking the scrolls and Khirbet Qumran, although the assumption is made by virtually everyone that the two are connected. This assumption stems from the evidence within the Dead Sea Scrolls themselves. One of the scrolls, called *The Manual of Discipline*, discloses the rules and reasons for the sect. Its teachings about bathing, baptism, and the like fit in well with the architecture and remains of Qumran. There is also the mention of Essene monastic communities on the western shore of the Dead Sea by Josephus, Pliny, and other Roman writers of that era.

It seems safe to say that here was a community of Jews living on the edge of the Dead Sea in an inaccessible place who were seeking out what living they could while they awaited the final work of God in history and the vindication of those who trusted in God, the Jews who remained true to the Torah.

The Book

Life in the Qumran community revolved around the Book. Divided into three sections—the Law, the Prophets, and the Writings—it was treasured and studied as the very oracles of God. Scribes and scholars, prophets and priests lived their lives in its pages. Those Jewish scribes wondered, dreamed, and prayed about the day, the kingdom, and the Messiah to come, hoping He would be a new David who would bring Israel to its eternal glory.

They were not alone, for every generation preceding them had studied and preserved, studied and preserved, studied and preserved the Book. Generation after generation had built painstaking commentary and layers of interpretation around its message.

The first and foremost of the three sections was the Torah, the Five Books of Moses, written three and a half millennia ago, with certain additions by his successors.

During the period of ancient Israel's greatest kings, David and Solomon, the writings of the Prophets began to take form. These were books of history and exhortation. They helped to interpret and apply the Law, or Torah, to the changing conditions of the First Commonwealth when Israel gained wealth and prominence.

During the age of Persian dominance, the Writings appeared. This included the books of poetry and wisdom, which applied the ancient Law to the needs and crises of the hour and made ever more sure the intent and goal of the ancient Word.

The Writings signaled the close of the Canon, the completion of the thirty-nine books of the Old Testament. However, other books were written that were hidden or reserved from the Sacred Canon. They were titled *Apocrypha* and used the names of the great sages of the time. Another collection, called the *Pseudepigrapha* or false-authored books, were written and attributed to such famous persons as Moses, Enoch, and Jeremiah.

The Qumran sect preserved and protected this enormous written tradition, applying it to their own time and situation. However, this was not the end of the drama of events to unfold on the northwest shore.

After the final fall of Jerusalem in A.D. 70, the Romans sent an expeditionary force down through this ancient desert. With incredible determination they spent three years destroying the last vestiges of independence and finally captured the nearly impregnable Masada. But a century later, revolution sparked into flame in this same wilderness. Through the centuries of Rome's decline, eerie brotherhoods and strange hermits preserved the Greek rites of Christianity here as well as the ancient texts.

In the seventh century after Christ, the hordes of Arabia, inflamed by the religion of Mohammed, passed by here on their way to the conquest of Constantinople. Several

Plate X
Location of the Qumran site and its proximity to Jerusalem.

centuries later the intrepid Crusaders traveled over the Roman roads until the European presence was settled on the desert. One army after another advanced and retreated along these shores. After centuries of Turkish rule, the British general Allenby and his Scots braved the gravel, sand, and heat to bring British rule to Palestine. And at last, in 1967, the Israeli Army, in one of history's greatest tank campaigns, drove out the armies of Jordan and raised the Star of David over this ancient inheritance of Abraham, the Land of the Book.

To understand Israel, Qumran, and the people that live there, we must understand the history of the Old Testament.

The Old Testament is the account of God's work on earth through His chosen people Israel and of all their trials and triumphs throughout history. The narrative begins with the call of Abraham from the city of Ur on the Euphrates and his journey to Canaan on the eastern shore of the Mediterranean Sea. There God gave to him the land from the mountains of Syria south to the Negev, the huge desert spreading down along the shores of the Dead Sea. Abraham was also given the promise that he would be the father of a great nation and that from that nation would come a blessing that would affect all mankind. These are the three aspects of the Old Testament revelation: the Promised Land, the chosen nation of Israel, and the promise of a universal blessing to come.

While the Jews have traditionally interpreted the blessing as the revelation of the Law in the Torah or the continuance of the Jewish people themselves, the Christian church has interpreted the blessing to be the coming of the Messiah, Jesus Christ, who died as a sacrifice and a fulfillment of the Law and thus brought atonement to all who believe in Him. This is the foundation of Christianity.

But in both Judaism and Christianity the Old Testament plays a significant and basic role. In fact, without the Old

Testament it is almost impossible to understand the New. The New Testament is the fulfillment and completion of the Old Testament revelation as it centers around the chosen people. The Old Testament was the primary religious and cultural document of Judaism. Exactly how it was produced and how the books were added to its collection is obscured by the mists of antiquity. It is known, however, that the Hebrew books have long been considered the authoritative oracles of God.

Conquests and Captivity

The nation of Israel and the Sacred Book passed through many periods of trial and tribulation. The Jews and the Bible were carried to many nations of the ancient world. After 600 B.C. small independent kingdoms were swallowed up by vast empires. First came the Assyro-Babylonian empire, which first carried Israel into captivity and later Judah in 586 B.C. Then the Jews returned to their ancient home under the friendly sovereignty of Persia. But under each conquest and dispersion more Jews were absorbed into the populations of other nations. During the time of Jeremiah in the eighth century B.C., many Jews migrated to Egypt and later to Persia and Anatolia. These displaced Jewish colonies lost the use of Hebrew and took on many of the customs and languages of the larger population among whom they lived.

The Book was carried, somewhat grudgingly, into the languages of these displaced Jews. Under the lordship of the Persian monarch Cyrus, the chief Semitic dialect of business and law was Aramaic, and the Jews had little choice but to adopt it as the official language of their court and commonwealth. Part of the book of the prophet Daniel, written during the Persian period, exists in Aramaic. The ancient Scriptures were translated into Aramaic in a form called "Targums." Many of the common people in the following centuries relied upon the Aramaic Targums for their spiritual nurture, for the ancient Hebrew had become all but incomprehensible. It frequently became useful to distinguish between the ancient biblical text and the commentaries on the text by writing the latter in Aramaic. The people of Palestine were still speaking Aramaic as their natural tongue when Jesus was born five hundred years later.

The Persians, with all of their archaic splendor, were the last of the oriental monarchies of antiquity. A new republican, anti-royalist spirit was abroad in the world. Its followers were called Hellenes, its leader was Alexander of Macedonia, and its language was Greek.

After a career of only fifteen years, Alexander was dead; but the ancient world had passed away and all of Asia was Greek in custom and in language, if not in heart. Many Jews resisted this tidal wave of Hellenism. Their corrupt court and temple hierarchy was supplanted in the everyday affairs of the people by a variety of sects. Each of these religious-political sects and parties looked to the ancient Scriptures for support and justification. Each alone claimed to rightly comprehend the oracles of God. Each produced its own school of interpretation and further enclosed the sacred text in concentric circles of tradition.

Of all the ancient states, each with its special religious hierarchy and tongue—the Babylonians, Hittites, Egyptians, Elamites, Canaanites, and Aryans—only the Jews survived the cultural shock of Hellenism. The rest perished and passed into oblivion. After Alexander's death in 323 B.C., his vast domain broke up into a number of semi-Greek states called the Hellenistic Kingdoms. The Jews thus passed under a line of rulers who held their seat in Antioch and who tortured thousands and killed hundreds of thousands of Jews and desecrated the temple on Mount Zion.

The overseas Jews succumbed to Greek just as their

forefathers had to Aramaic. There is also some evidence that the Hellenistic rulers had some curiosity about the Jewish Holy Book. For whatever reason, the Jews made a translation of their Scriptures into Greek. This version of the ancient Word was known as the Septuagint. Ancient copies and fragments of the Septuagint have been unearthed in many locations throughout the deserts of Egypt and the Sinai peninsula. The Septuagint was the major Bible version of the intertestamental period, the four hundred years between the Old and New Testament.

Certain versions of the Septuagint were translated from Hebrew manuscripts that were older and more authentic than the standard Hebrew Bibles of later ages. Unlike all of the languages of the ancient religious-states, Greek was written in an alphabet of only twenty-four symbols or letters. It provided easy literacy for the common man. A new Hellenistic dialect of Greek came into being, called "koiné" or "common," and it became the everyday speech of business and commerce from the Balkans to the Ganges River.

It also appears that the Persians, and the Greeks who succeeded them, were fascinated with the ancient religion of Israel. Because of its transcendental nature, that is, because it exalted a God who was supreme and above all of human experience and because it did not have idols and immoral pagan rites, the Persians and the Greeks were respectful of it. It was because of the universality of Koiné Greek that the New Testament was written in Koiné Greek and that most of the quotations of the Old Testament used in the New Testament are taken from the Septuagint. Ultimately, the Septuagint became the exclusive version of the Old Testament used by the early Christian church. Through this translation of the Old Testament, the Law of Moses and the history of Israel became available to Greeks and Romans and thus prepared the way for the missionaries of Jesus Christ two centuries later.

The Scrolls at Qumran

This brief but important review of the history of the Old Testament helps explain the mixture of languages and cultural references found in the Dead Sea Scrolls. The process of preservation, copying, and publication that has gone on since the Qumran discovery has been a slow and laborious process.

In the thirty years since the discovery of the Dead Sea Scrolls, a large number of the full scrolls and a great many fragments have been published and deciphered. They did not seem to give us any New Testament material, but their value for Old Testament studies has been phenomenal. Before the scrolls were found, the very earliest Old Testament manuscripts were dated to about A.D. 900. These were derived from the Medieval Jewish centers in Southern Russia, and the text they provided was fairly uniform and of little variation from much later printed versions from Western Europe. But the Dead Sea Scrolls from Qumran bring us one thousand years closer to the original text, to as early as 150 B.C.!

The original excavators at Qumran found a number of caves dotting the high escarpment around the wadi or dry creek bed, below the ruin. As mentioned earlier, it was thought that this ruin, about one hundred feet in length, was the remains of a Roman fort or outpost.

The character and contents of Qumran had not been totally lost in antiquity. Several ancient writers mentioned the Qumran area, the community, and the scrolls present there. Josephus wrote of the Essenes. Also, an ancient narrative speaks of a Septuagint version of the Psalms recovered from a jar near Jericho and used by the church father, Origen. There is also evidence that the Medieval sect of the Karaite Jews may have studied and preserved some of the nonbiblical texts that had been recovered from the Qumran caves and that were subsequently lost again in the turbidity of history. In the

Plate XI
The entrances to many of the caves are small and once unsealed are susceptible to rapid erosion.

last years of the nineteenth century, similar fragments were recovered from the "book repository," or *Genizah*, of the Old Cairo synagogue in Egypt.

A Survey of the Scrolls

Enough of the material from Qumran has now been recovered and published that a brief survey of the materials can be made. There are first and foremost a large number of whole scrolls and fragments of biblical books. All of the books of the Old Testament are thus far represented with the exception of Esther.

Cave 1 contained two scrolls of Isaiah, one complete and the other damaged. There was also a commentary on Habakkuk, a series of sectarian documents, and the *Scroll of the War of the Sons of Light against the Sons of Darkness*, which gives a very detailed and complex plan for the order of battle of the sectarian Jews in their last great apocalyptic struggle against the heathen and the infidels of Rome. This fascinating book has parallels with passages in 2 Peter, Jude, and Revelation. It shows that the immediate concern of the authors of the work was the approaching end of the world. Along with this apocryphal piece was located a pair of purely tutorial works for the operation of the community. One, the *Manual of Discipline*, has already been described (page 53). The other was called *Hymns of Thanksgiving* and contained a sort of running paraphrase on the biblical Psalms, which were most likely chanted by the community. Along with these longer works, Cave 1 contained fragments of seventy or more other works of the intertestamental period.

Cave 2 yielded part of a copy of the apocryphal book of Jubilees, a description of the apocalyptic Jerusalem in the Aramaic language, and a number of biblical and apocryphal fragments.

In *Cave 3* were found several hundred fragments in He-

Plate XII and XIII
Entrances to a large and a small cave.

brew and Aramaic and two copper scrolls. These strange documents contained information on the amounts and whereabouts of a fabulous treasure. They were the greatest challenge to those unrolling and publishing the material.

Cave 4 is easily visible from the ruins of the monastic dwelling. It is at the top of a narrow ridge that juts out into the wadi, which is hundreds of feet below its sheer rock sides. The inaccessibility kept its secret inviolate for two thousand years.

From *Cave 4* has come the largest number of fragments yet uncovered. The majority is yet to be published. However, preliminary reports state that there are fragments in the ancient Hebrew "round" script of Genesis, Exodus, and Job. Fragments of more than fourteen different manuscript copies of Deuteronomy and fragments of other biblical books with texts similar to the Septuagint were found there. It is estimated that nearly five hundred different titles may be preserved in fragmentary form. *Caves 5 and 6* contained more fragments but in lesser quantity than the thousands of pieces from *Cave 4*.

The Qumran Copyists

Although there is still some debate as to whether all of the vast library at Qumran actually was written in the tiny rooms of those buildings, it is clear that some conclusions about the authors and preservers can be drawn.

The library was not that of the official, established Jerusalem hierarchy. A number of passages in the scrolls are highly critical of the profaning of the temple by the contemporary administration that cooperated with the Roman military.

The copyists were seeking to interpret the whole of the Old Testament in light of their own situation. All of the prophecies were taken to have two meanings: the prior one relating to the time when the original book was written, and a latter one referring to the age and circumstances of the sectarian community.

Plate XIV
Visible from the ruins of Qumran, Cave 4 contained the largest mass
of fragments yet uncovered.

Truth was held fully and uniquely by the community. Although small, the community believed it would soon be vindicated in the approaching apocalypse when God would restore Israel. The Scriptures were hedged or fenced about in their very wording by commentary and precise interpretation of the words and their pronunciation. The writings of the sages of the past were all of value in understanding the biblical texts. But while the Qumran community was engaged in biblical intepretation and disciplined living, a powerful political force entered the stage of history.

The Romans

A bare generation before Jesus was born, the Roman Empire was founded by its first and probably greatest emperor, Caesar Augustus. He was the nephew of Julius Caesar, and he united all the vast and disparate areas of Roman control under one central authority. He was a man of great ability and of singular learning who knew both Greek and Latin. He built upon the Greek tradition in the East. Interestingly enough, Greek remained the language of commerce and travel well into the third century of the Roman era. The Romans, however, established something that the Greek kingdoms could never have brought about: political stability. While there were frequent revolutions and many wars, much of the Roman Empire was in a state of tranquility, even if that tranquility was mixed with slavery and barbarism. The sheer power of Rome threatened the very survival of Judaism even more than the onslaught of Hellenism had done.

But the Roman Empire is the indispensible background against which the scenes of the Incarnation and the life of Christ were acted out. And it is also against a background of Jewish national hope based on an interpretation of the ancient

Plate XV
Emperor Caesar Augustus

Scriptures that the formation of the New Testament can best be understood.

The New Testament was written soon after the last remnants of Alexander's once vast empire were obliterated and the Roman Empire was established. The Roman system was the first great unitary organization of government that spanned cultures, races, and religions. It gave the first glimpse of the incredible power and stupendous wealth that lay in the capacity of the common man, the citizen soldier, and the popular politician. The Romans applied the objectivity of Greek science and technology to the market place and consequently amassed wealth and power greater than the wildest dreams of any king or pharaoh of the ancient world.

Josephus, the Romanized Jewish historian, reported that the conflict between the pragmatic and pagan Romans and the pious and ordered Jews was long and violent. The repeated attempts by the Romans to reduce the political system of Judea to Roman puppetry was met with insurrection and bloodshed. Romans were assassinated and Jews were crucified. Many Jews turned their backs on their puppet Jewish monarchs and the hired tax collectors of Rome and sought strength in the sects that were abroad in the land and eager to gain adherents.

A renewed interest in the Scriptures brought about two phenomena. One was the continued encirclement of the Torah, the Five Books of Moses, with finer and more exacting interpretation. This process ultimately yielded the Mishnah and Talmud. The second was the change in Jewish worship from the sacerdotal rituals and the rites of the great temple in Jerusalem to the study of the Torah and the examination of the Scriptures in the local synogogues that were found in every village and hamlet inhabited by Jews, both in Israel and abroad.

The notion was everywhere that the long ages of the Jewish

state were drawing to a close, and that God Himself was about to do a new thing for His people.

In contrast to the intricacies of the sects of the time, the group around Jesus of Nazareth was uncomplicated and guileless. When His disciples wrote their experiences based upon His life and teachings, their recollections were by nature episodic and straightforward. But one thing they had in common with all other Jewish religious communities was that they built upon the words of Moses and the prophets. As a matter of fact, they simply followed their Master and His custom of more closely defining the meaning of the Old Testament.

However, with the teachings of Jesus a new and different element was present—the authority of the Messiah, the servant of God. Unlike the rabbinical and sectarian teachers of the time, Jesus' deeds were revelation itself. He fulfilled all of the Old Testament expectations in one career and opened a new epoch in God's revelation and plan of redemption.

4
The Fragments From Cave 7

CAVE 7 was discovered in mid-March 1955. It lay nearly a mile to the north of Khirbet Qumran, on a different ridge. The entrance into the cave was a tiny opening in the rock only four-and-a-half by six feet. The discoverers were trained archaeologists. There was no evidence that any of the local Arabs had previously discovered, much less entered, the cave. The area was still under Jordanian control, and unfortunately many details of the discovery were not recorded and are now unknown.

There are no photographs of Cave 7 and no architectural drawings showing the position of the material in the cave as it was actually found. Neither were there what archaeologists call *in situ* photographs. Eyewitnesses of the opening of the cave stated it was sealed in A.D. 70 and all the fragments date from no later than A.D. 60. However, it must be remembered that the whole of the excavation and recovery of the Dead Sea Scrolls and their final distribution was conducted during wartime, in a region of incredible terrain, and under the guns of both combatants. Cave 7 was so small that the efforts to excavate it opened it to erosion so that it no longer exists.

Inside Cave 7 were the remains of two large jars, one with

Hebrew letters that may be transcribed ROME written on the top shoulder, once on each side of the jar. Fragments of other jars, similar to those found in the ruins of Khirbet Qumran, were also found. Some scholars sought to identify the letters on the jar with the name of some person; however, it seems clear that Rome, the ruling center of the world at that time, is the most probable reference, and that the jars came from there.

On the clay floor of the cave, apparently near the larger pots, were found eighteen tiny scraps of papyri and six imprinted clods of clay where some ancient papyri had all but passed into dust through the centuries, leaving the stain and imprint of some of their letters.

There are three aspects in which the small fragments from Cave 7 are absolutely unique from all of the other finds at Qumran:

(1) All the fragments are exclusively in Greek; none are in Hebrew or Aramaic.

(2) They are all of papyrus, the ancient paper made from stems of reeds. Almost all of the other texts and fragments from Qumran are of parchment, the prepared skins of animals.

(3) All have writing on only one side of the papyrus sheet, which means they were pieces of a scroll rather than pages from a book or codex.

Faced with the enormous number of finds and the incredible age of so much of the Hebrew material, the discoverers of Cave 7 made no special attempt to rush into print with their finds. After being discovered, the fragments were allowed to lie on open tables in damaging sunlight under the rather lax administration of the Jordan Department of Antiquities.

The finds from what were called the "small caves," which

included Caves 2, 3, 5, 6, 7, 8, 9, and 10 were all published in two volumes in 1962, nearly a decade after their discovery. They were prepared and edited by three distinguished French scholars, all connected with the authoritative École Biblique et Archéologique Française that is housed in an imposing old stone building directly across from one of the gates of the Old City of Jerusalem. The three editors were: M. Baillet, J. T. Milik, and R. de Vaux.

The two volumes were published as *Discoveries in the Judaean Desert, III*, with the French subtitle "Les 'Petites Grottes' de Qumran." (The "Small Caves" of Qumran.) They were produced by Oxford University at Clarendon Press in England and the text is entirely in French. The first volume contains 317 pages of transliterations; that is, the ancient texts were printed in modern characters with the interpretations of difficult letters and the comments of the editors. The material from Cave 7 fills only four pages—142–145.

The two largest fragments from Cave 7, numbered 1 and 2, were identified. Number 1 is a portion of the Septuagint, Exodus 28: 4–7. The fragment preserves parts of nineteen lines. It was noted by the editors that the text left out verse 5 which is in the standard Hebrew text, an interesting variant.

Fragment number 2 was identified as a portion of an apocryphal letter, that is, a work purporting to be biblical but not accepted as such. It is from the "Letter of Jeremiah," but again there is a variant from the better known texts of the work. In this case, parts of five lines are preserved. In all, twenty-two letters can be made out on fragment 2; however, five are questionable and are marked as such with a small dot printed under them, the standard practice of papyrologists.

The editors note two other distinctive characteristics of the fragments from Cave 7:

(1) They were written in the earlier Greek style of handwriting known as uncial, a capital letter form

developed from Greek inscriptions on stones and characteristic of texts before the fifth century A.D. But the editors add another note: the precise style of uncial is an uncommon one, discovered by a twentieth-century German expert on Greek writing styles, Schubart. He called the style *Zierstil* or "decorative," a fact that has vast importance as we shall see.

(2) The fragments are dated by no less an authority than the British scholar C. H. Roberts as being within the first century after Christ. In fact the bracketed dates, the earliest and latest, have been set even narrower for some of the fragments.

The second volume of *Discoveries in the Judaean Desert, III* is a thin album of seventy-one photographic plates. The originals were taken a decade before publication with inferior equipment and under less than ideal conditions. The Clarendon Press reproduced them in a sort of sepia on nonglossy, off-white paper. Many of the reproductions would be unreadable without the editor's notes in the first volume (see Plate III).

At the bottom of page 143 of the commentary volume of *Discoveries* there is a most intriguing title (in French):

"Fragments not identified"

and below that an even more fascinating subtitle:

"3–5. Biblical Texts?"

The all important ingredient is the question mark. On the following two pages each tiny fragment is transcribed, with many letters marked by the dot showing uncertainty. Fragment 5 has a short paragraph of introduction, again mentioning the *Zierstil* style, and giving the precise date 50 B.C. to A.D. 50.

Unfortunately, Plate XXX (see p. 19), on which all of the fragments from Cave 7 are published, is particularly unreadable because of dark shadows, blurs, and lines obscuring the letters on the tiny fragments. The editors gave extensive suggestions for reading various obscure letters but were unable to propose a reading or citation for any one of the sixteen fragments.

The two volumes of *Discoveries* are certainly not rare; in fact, they are commonly found in most university and seminary libraries. Undoubtedly, thousands of students and professors leafed through the pages in the following decade, and many must have wondered from which part of the Septuagint the fragments came. But the fragments were so small and indistinct that apparently no one was intrigued enough to try to solve the mystery. After all, there were more important things to be studied and greater discoveries to be made elsewhere! Or so scholars must have thought.

5
José O'Callaghan

WHILE SCHOLARS in Europe and America wrote hundreds of books and thousands of articles on various aspects of the Dead Sea Scrolls, not one jot or tittle appeared on the small fragments from Cave 7; the fragments lay as dormant and unnoticed in the Rockefeller Museum as they had on the floor of the tiny cave less than forty miles away. The fact that the official publication of these fragments was in French and that the plates were of such poor quality further obscured their true nature.

If we were to stage this drama of the tiny fragments, we would here insert a direction something like "Enter the laughing Spaniard" for that is exactly what happened. A decade after the fragments in Cave 7 were discovered—and a further decade after they were published—a scholar-detective finally identified the incredible little pieces of ancient text. But who in the world is Father O'Callaghan, and how did he make his identification?

José O'Callaghan was born in Spain on October 7, 1922. He demonstrated his scholarly propensity at an early age and became a Jesuit, earning the licentiate in philosophy and theology. He later earned a doctorate in philosophy at the University of Madrid and another doctorate in the classics at the University of Milan. He speaks French, Italian, and English as well as Spanish and is a master of the classical languages and German. He became Professor of Greek Literature at the University of Madrid in 1957. In 1970 he was appointed Professor of Greek Papyrology at the University of Barcelona. In 1971 he was appointed Professor of Greek Papyrology and Paleography at the world-renowned Pontifical Biblical Institute in Rome, where he is now a professor.

In addition, he is a scientific collaborator at the Faculty of Theology at San Cugat del Valles in Barcelona. At that institution he is also curator of a very important collection of ancient papyri from Egypt and the Middle East (PPalau Rib.), numbering more than two thousand items. Of this fund of ancient manuscripts, the most important that have been published thus far are the Gospels of Mark and Luke in Sahidic, a Coptic dialect. They are the only two complete Gospels presently preserved, and they are also the oldest in the world. Their antiquity goes back to the early fifth century. The hand in which they are written is reminiscent of the beauty of the famous *Vaticanus* and *Sinaiticus* codices. They were published by Professor Hans Quecke, a colleague of O'Callaghan at the Biblical Institute in Rome. Dr. O'Callaghan is also editor of the scholarly journal *Studia Papyrologica* and the author of a number of books and more than one hundred articles.

David Estrada met Father O'Callaghan in Barcelona in 1972 and wrote in detail of that meeting and of O'Callaghan's discovery in the June 1972 issue of *Eternity* Magazine. William White, Jr., has corresponded with O'Callaghan continually since 1972. The two finally met in the spring of 1977 in Rome:

Only a block or so from the enormous tomb of Vittorio Immanuel, there is a short, narrow street. Along one side is the imposing wall of the famed Gregorian University; opposite is building number 35—a high masonry building housing the equally famous Pontifical Biblical Institute.

White knocked on the enormous wooden door in vain; then he saw a bronze doorbell. Upon pushing it, an electric bell echoed deep within the massive walls. An elderly porter opened the door and asked whom he wished to see. After telling him, White was invited in and shown to a small sitting room off the narrow corridor.

After only five minutes, the sound of a man's laughter and quick footsteps echoed down the hall. In another minute the door of the small waiting room swung open and a husky, gray-haired man literally ran in and seized the visitor by the shoulders. There followed gales of laughter and a torrent of accented English: "Oh, Dr. White, my friend. I am so very glad at last to meet you, my colleague. It is such a pleasure!" The two instantly became friends. There followed a number of sessions in the professor's well-equipped study where most of the technical discussions were taped as background for this book.

Father O'Callaghan is a vital and charming person with long years of expertise in his chosen field. He is a careful, quiet scholar and certainly not the type of man to play to the headlines. The elder statesman of American New Testament scholars, Bruce M. Metzger, formerly of Princeton Theological Seminary, assessed him as "an accomplished papyrologist whose previous publications have been characterized by scholarly insight and balanced judgment."

Ever since 1958, O'Callaghan has published his finds in the field of papyrology. He has used the generally accepted methods of dating, deciphering, and identifying papyri. In the fourteen years between the appearance of his first article and the announcement of his identification of the Qumran fragments, he had successfully identified many classical and biblical papyri. Among the classical authors, he has identified fragments of the writings of Democritus, Homer, Herodotus, Ovid, Theocritus, and Plato. In addition, he has worked with most of the world's great papyrus collections: Bodmer, Yale, British Museum, Berlin Museum, National Museum Naples, and many, many others.

He is considered by many to be the foremost authority on the writing of the sacred names in Greek papyri and Latin manuscripts. There is no doubt of his firm position as a leading scholar in this intensely difficult field. O'Callaghan does not approach his work with evangelical presuppositions and the hope of discovering an early-dated New Testament. Instead he is an oustanding papyrologist of Roman Catholic tradition, who in his course of study happened upon some startling evidence. To make certain that his New Testament identifications of the fragments were correct, O'Callaghan studied the actual fragments at the Rockefeller Museum in Jerusalem in April 1972. This is a fact the authors have verified with Israeli officials.

6

How Can We Be Sure?

FRAGMENT 5—the first one that O'Callaghan identified from Cave 7—is a small piece of papyrus that contains nine certain letters and ten uncertain ones. How can we be sure that O'Callaghan's identification is the right one, especially since the correct identification of these nineteen small letters could, according to the *Chicago Tribune*, revolutionize biblical research?

Trying to identify an ancient fragment is like pulling a small piece of paper with printing on it out of a fire and trying to figure out what book and page the paper came from. It may seem like an impossible task, but it is a simple matter of scholarly detective work.

The first thing that will concern the papyrologist is the age of the fragment. There are many methods used for determining this information—carbon-14 dating, examining the kind of writing, and dating some of the artifacts found with the fragment—and several different methods are apt to be used on each fragment. In the case of the fragments found in Cave 7, however, the determination of the age of the fragments was made by Israeli archaeologists before the identification was made, and the dates have never seriously been called into question.

The next concern is to determine what the letters actually are that appear on the fragment. Letters that are distinct and whole are relatively easy to identify with certainty. But papyrologists will state that a letter exists when even the smallest trace of it appears and they will try to identify it. It is remarkable how much can be determined from just a small portion of a letter. For instance, if a fragment contained **COA⁻**, the letters "COA" are certain, followed by a fourth letter that is uncertain. What is left of the fourth letter is a very short horizontal line at the top with no indication of a vertical line to the left. However, "T" and "Z" are the only letters that contain a horizontal line at the top without a left-hand-side vertical line underneath it, as in "E." The fourth letter is uncertain, but probably a "T," and the word is likely to be "COAT." This could be confirmed by the context.

Suggestions for uncertain letters can be considered plausible if they make sense in the context of what can be seen. Of course, a letter fragment can indicate two or three or even more possibilities. But once an identification has been proposed, the uncertain letters must be confirmed by the identification, or alternate suggestions for the uncertain letters must be made that *will remain true to the remnants while conforming to the identification*. In the example given, it would be difficult to accept an identification that required reading the word as "COAL" because "L" is not true to the remnant of the letter that we can see.

Obviously, not even the most astute papyrologist is going to be able to achieve one hundred percent accuracy in his suggestions for incomplete and indistinct letters. If and when an identification is made, he must be prepared to consider some alternative possibilities for the letters that are difficult to read.

As with the dating, the determination of the letters on the fragments from Cave 7 was made before O'Callaghan made his identification. Thus there was not the temptation to make a determination of the letters to fit a preconceived idea of what the fragment should read.

One of the basic principles in trying to identify a fragment is that the lines of a proposed identification must fit a particular stichometry, or the number of letters in each line. Ancient texts have several stylistic features, one of the most important being that the number of characters in the lines of a given text are approximately the same, and variations rarely exceed ten percent of the total of the line. The same principle applies to printed texts, such as this book, today. For example, if the lines of a text have an average of twenty-two characters, no line will have more than twenty-four or less than twenty unless there is a semantic or a grammatical necessity to exceed the line. Any extra letters are often written in smaller characters so as to accommodate the line to the space available.

With this principle in mind, we can illustrate the validity of O'Callaghan's identification by means of an experiment. Take a New Testament, close your eyes, and open it at random. Now with your eyes still closed, place your finger on one of the pages. Open your eyes and note the three letters on each of the three lines above your finger. I have done this and the letters are as follows:

	I	II	III
Line 1	d	e	a
Line 2	r	i	t
Line 3	.	l	a

Now try to find another passage with the letters "d" and "r" above the "space" (marked with a dot). Then find an "e" next to a "d" and above an "i" and so on through the whole group of nine letters, one of which is a "space."

I found this particular arrangement of letters in *The Open*

Bible edition of the King James Version. The text is Revelation 20, the last part of verse 14 through the middle of verse 15. The nine letters are underlined:

> ¹⁴And death and hell were cast into the
> lake of fire. This is the second d̲e̲a̲th.
> ¹⁵And whosoever was not found w̲r̲i̲t̲t̲e̲n in
> the book of life was cast into the ̲l̲a̲k̲e̲ of fire.

Now look for this same nine letters in the same arrangement elsewhere! But be warned—you may read through thousands of pages and never find it. The chances of finding it are astronomical unless you come across the identical passage in an identical edition of the Bible with which you started. Try this experiment in your Sunday school class or your Bible study group and you will see how difficult it really is.

When we recall that fragment 5 contains a matrix of nineteen letters distributed from seven to three characters over five lines, we can see that the coincidence of finding even a close approximation of the same arrangement of letters— that is, by allowing a shift in the lines due to stichometry— results in odds in the millions unless the Mark 6:52,53 passage is chosen.

We can see the development of some of these problems and procedures by looking at a concrete example: the identification of the less controversial fragments 1 and 2. These two fragments, in spite of difficulties, have been firmly identified as passages from Exodus and the Letter of Jeremiah. If they can be identified, why can not fragment 5 and its companions?

A number of scholars have protested that fragment 5 is too "dim" or "indistinct" to be deciphered adequately (see Plate XVI). Others have claimed that even if the deciphering is granted, there is too little of the text available to establish a firm identification. What is the actual situation?

By comparing the photos of fragments 1, 2, and 5, the layman can see for himself that such charges simply are not

Plate XVI
Fragment 5

85

true (see Plates XVII and XVIII). Fragment 5 is as clear as fragment 1, much clearer than fragment 2, and is almost equal to 2 in the number of readable characters.

Nevertheless, in an exclusive *New York Times* article, one leading scholar charged that fragment 5 was "indistinct." The assertion came from Pierre Benoit, director of the École Biblique et Archèologique Française in Jerusalem. Benoit was one of the Greek experts who worked on the deciphering of the Cave 7 fragments as presented in *Discoveries*. Benoit, a French Dominican, was identified in the *Times* story as a "colleague" of O'Callaghan, which in the strict sense of the word is not so. Benoit might have been considerably more friendly if he were truly associated with O'Callaghan, but the two men are separated at least by the length of the Mediterranean Sea as well as by historic differences in their religious orders.

Taken at face value, Benoit's comments make O'Callaghan look ridiculous. Benoit said that as soon as he saw the article in *Biblica* he went "immediately to the Rockefeller Museum in Jerusalem, where the original scroll fragments are held." In addition to noting the indistinct character of the letters, Benoit pointedly stated that O'Callaghan had only worked with "photocopies" rather than the original fragments and, most damaging of all, "one spot that showed up in the photocopies as a possible part of a Greek letter in Father O'Callaghan's reading turned up in the original fragment to be merely a hole in the papyrus."

These testy remarks are as absurd as they are unkind. In the first place, the term "photocopies" conjures up in the layman's mind some kind of inferior, nonauthoritative product. But, of course, no reliable scholar would think of working with nonauthoritative material. Benoit undoubtedly realized that O'Callaghan worked from the text and photos published in *Discoveries*, but when he used the term "photocopies" he definitely created a false impression in the minds of most *Times* readers.

Plate XVII
Fragment 1

Plate XVIII
Fragment 2

In the second place, what basis was there for suggesting the idea that O'Callaghan read a hole in the fragment as "a possible part of a Greek letter"? O'Callaghan did no such thing.

As a matter of fact, for all practical purposes, O'Callaghan followed the readings given by the editors of *Discoveries*, and one of these editors was Benoit himself. In the case of James 1: 23,24, fragment 8, and Mark 4:28, fragment 6, which are the other two fragments discussed in *Biblica*, O'Callaghan accepted the *Discoveries* decipherments as is. That leaves only fragment 5 as the focal point of Benoit's disparaging remark about reading a hole as a letter-part.

So what is the case with O'Callaghan's reading of fragment 5? First of all, he asked for no change in the reading of the nine distinct, whole letters. Furthermore, he followed the original suggestions of the editors on four of the partial ones. The fact is, O'Callaghan has not in any way dismissed any of the editors' certain readings.

To see what is acceptable according to scholarly standards, look closely at fragment 1. It consists of a larger piece containing seven lines, with traces of lines above and below these seven lines—nine lines in all—plus a smaller piece showing one line and traces of the line above. Note in particular the tiny traces of letters on lines 1 and 9 of the larger piece and the traces on line 1 of the smaller piece. Despite the extreme fragmentary nature of these letter remnants, the editors of *Discoveries* were able to offer suggestions for two letters on line 1, three letters on line 9, and three letters on line 1 of the smaller piece.

Next, note the letter-remnants at the beginning and end of line 4. This is the line that shows the three letters in the center **ΧΡΥ**. The *Discoveries'* editors offer suggestions for these fragmentary letters at the ends of the line. The editors also offer readings for the last letter of line 5, for the first letter of line 6, for the letter that just barely begins after the **Κ** on line

7, and for the first letter of line 8. In every case, so little is seen on the fragment that considerable finesse was required on the part of the transcribers.

The point of this examination is *not* to show that the original editors were inaccurate or reckless. With each difficult letter they either took their clues from the context of the passage *after* the identification was made, or they did some very astute deciphering.

What is obvious in studying fragment 1 is that suggestions for uncertain letters can be considered plausible if they can be reconciled to what can be seen—*even if what can be seen is extremely limited.* When an identification of a fragment is suggested, it is frequently necessary to reconsider and adopt alternative possibilities for some of the letters that are difficult to read.

That is precisely the situation we now have with fragment 5. O'Callaghan suggested an identification that agrees with nine certain letters and six out of ten of the uncertain ones. O'Callaghan is only asking that the remaining four letters be seen as different letters than the *Discoveries'* editors first imagined. His critics cannot maintain that the fragmentary letters cannot possibly read as O'Callaghan suggests since they offered no alternative reading. The primary determiner must be a successful alternative identification.

But what about the charge that there is insufficient text in fragment 5 for a firm identification? It is necessary to make a comparison of fragment 5 with fragment 2. According to the editors of *Discoveries*, fragment 2 offers seventeen clearly decipherable or "certain" letters. In addition, we find suggestions for five uncertain letters.

But on close examination we can hardly help but see that fragment 2 does not really offer seventeen certain letters. If we approach it objectively, as one is forced to approach a still-unidentified fragment, surely not more than twelve letters are certain. Thus we really have before us a fragment

Plate XIX
Papyrus 9

with twelve certain letters and ten uncertain letters. By comparison, fragment 5 offers ten uncertain letters also.

The point of this comparison is clear: If a fragment of twenty-two letters, ten of which are uncertain, is not too small to be firmly identified, then a similar fragment containing twenty letters surely is not too small to be identified. This contention becomes even stronger when one notices that, overall, fragment 5 is much easier to read than fragment 2. "Indistinct" can be applied to fragment 2, but it is not appropriate in the case of fragment 5.

It has been pointed out that many, many texts have been identified from far less evidence than fragment 5. A particularly fine example is Papyrus 9 (see Plate XIX), accepted in the official list of papyri by Aland and all other scholars. O'Callaghan discusses the indentification of this fragmentary text:

> P9 is similar to 7Q5 in that it also consists of only five lines, albeit with over three times as many letters. It has been identified with 1 John 4:11,12 by everyone. But it badly garbles a word in the first line, misspells a word in the second, omits a word and misspells another in the third and adds a nonsense word in the fourth (line 5 is all right). If only the first four or five letters of each line were preserved (instead of twelve or thirteen) I doubt that it would have been identified, or the suggestion of 1 John 4:11,12 accepted.[1]

O'Callaghan also gives the examples of fragments of Homer and Menander, which contain half as many visible letters as fragment 5 and yet were identified with certainty. Even Fitzmyer candidly wrote, "This meager state of affairs is not encouraging, but the trained papyrologist has learned to work with less."[2]

---

[1]Wilbur N. Pickering, *The Identity of the New Testament Text*, (Nashville: Thomas Nelson Inc., Publishers, 1977) p. 148.
[2]"A Qumran Fragment of Mark?" *America*, June 24, 1972, p. 647.

7
Details of the Discovery

BECAUSE OF the extreme importance of the fragments from Cave 7, it is necessary to look at each fragment and each identification and the accompanying evidence. It is our contention that the amazing evidence speaks for itself.

The archaeologists who discovered Cave 7 found a total of eighteen papyrus fragments plus a calcified portion of earth in three pieces with a reverse image imprinted on it, apparently because one of the fragments, number 18, was in prolonged, face-down contact with the earth. The original editors of *Discoveries* identified two of the fragments, and O'Callaghan has identified eight more (actually nine, for *Discoveries* shows number 6 as two pieces, each of which represents a different New Testament book). That leaves eight that are still unidentified. Of these, only fragment 3 and the earth impression seem to offer promise of ever being identified; very few letters can be deciphered on the others (see Plate XX).

Fragment 5

O'Callaghan began with fragment number 5 and identified it as Mark 6:52,53 (see Plate XVI, p. 85):

(They had not) understood about the loaves, but their minds were closed, and they finished the crossing and came to Gennesaret where they made fast.

The arrangement of the English represents both the word order of the Greek and the actual state of preservation of the fragment. It does not read easily in English, but it is the clearest approximation of what actually exists on the fragments.

In our rough approximation of the text as it would appear in English, it can be seen to fit the original page very well with the number of letters in each line falling into a stichometry equal to that of fragment 1.[1] The Greek will be seen to fit even more accurately with the large gap before the AND which begins verse 53.

The following diagram shows the reading of the original editors as it appeared in *Discoveries* (Column I), the reading by O'Callaghan (Column II), the restructuring of the lines as

I	II
].[	[συνηκαν]ε̣[πιτοισαρτοισ]
]. τῳ α̣.[	[αλληνα]υ̣τωνη[καρδιαπεπωρω]
]η και τῳ[	[μεν]η. καιτι[απερασαντεσ]
εγε]γνησ[εν	[ηλθονεισε]γνησ[αρετκαι]
]θ̣η̣ε̣σ[	[προσωρμισ]θησα̣[νκαιεξελ]

III	IV
[συνηκαν] ἐ[πίτοις ἄρτοις,]	20 letters
[·ἀλλ·ἠν α]·υτῶν ἠ [καρσία πεπωρω–]	23 letters
[μέν]η. Καὶ τι[απεράσαντες]	20 letters
[ἦλθον εἰς Γε]γνησ[αρὲτ καὶ]	21 letters
[προσωρμίσ]θησα̣]ν καὶ ἐξελ–]	21 letters

[1]A reconstruction of each fragment in English follows the chart of Greek letters. These reconstructions are difficult to match to any English text because they follow the actual Greek words on the fragments and are impossible to read directly into our familiar English versions. But they do show very accurately what exists on each fragment.

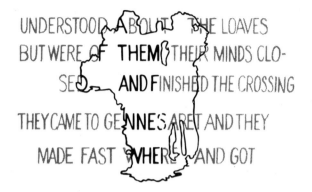

UNDERSTOOD ABOUT THE LOAVES
BUT WERE OF THEM THEIR MINDS CLO-
SED AND FINISHED THE CROSSING
THEY CAME TO GENNESARET AND THEY
MADE FAST WHERE AND GOT

in a modern printed Greek text (Column III), and the number of letters per line as proposed by O'Callaghan (Column IV). We will treat each of the fragments that follow in this same way.

Of course, the strength of O'Callaghan's identification depends first of all on how he reads the letters on the fragment. If he hopelessly departs from the transcription of the scholars who first worked on it, the proposed identification is worthless.

Brackets indicate the boundaries of the fragment. Actually, there is more to the fragment on the right side, but the area is so damaged and distorted that little or nothing can be detected. A dot under a letter means it is incomplete or faint and cannot be read with certainty. But one should consult the editors' footnotes in *Discoveries* to learn how confident they feel about the transcription of each uncertain letter. A dot alone, with no letter above it, means that only a trace of the letter is visible and the editors do not wish to "force" the transcription by offering a specific reading. Again, however, the editors' footnotes may make one or more suggestions as to what the letter might be.

Note particularly the letters O'Callaghan considers certain, the ones without dots under them. There are ten, including one that *Discoveries* shows as uncertain. The rest are acknowledged by O'Callaghan to be uncertain. An accurate count of O'Callaghan's certain letters and their correlation to those identified as certain in *Discoveries* is important, inasmuch as one European scholar charges that O'Callaghan "positively identifies the imperfect, the defective, and the illegible letters, and accords to them the same degree of reliability as to the nine perfect ones. . . ." This statement is obviously false.

The only discrepancies between O'Callaghan and *Discoveries* regarding the transcription of certain letters occur in the second line, where O'Callaghan removes the dot from under the third letter. In the latter case, instead of taking the editors' first choice, **Є**, O'Callaghan prefers their second choice, **C**. He explains by underlining the observation they themselves make in their footnote about the letter: the middle stroke of the **Є** is not certain.

Even though O'Callaghan has removed the dot under this letter, he adds a qualifying comment, "The **C** is nearly certain." In other words, O'Callaghan does not claim absolute certainty; and in any case, he has stayed within the legitimate choices the editors themselves give for the letter.

But what about the ten uncertain letters the editors indicate on fragment 5? How closely does O'Callaghan follow them in regard to these?

He agrees with them in six cases and offers new readings in four. The other agreements are: the lettertrace—a faint outline of a letter—on line 1, the first letter of lines 3, 4, and 5, and the last letter of line 4.

The area of disagreement, then, is confined to four letters: the last two letters of line 2, the last letter of line 3, and the last letter of line 5. Regarding the latter, almost nothing appears on the fragment, making it all but impossible to argue for either O'Callaghan or *Discoveries*. For the final letter of line 3, O'Callaghan's **I** is just as plausible as the *Discoveries* **ω**, since only one vertical stroke is preserved.

Plate XX
Fragment 3

This leaves only two letters: O'Callaghan's **NH** on line 2, versus *Discoveries'* **Δ**. There are rather technical arguments for and against both readings, which we cannot give space to here. But we believe O'Callaghan's reading is plausible, provided one allows the possibility that the diagonal stroke and right vertical leg of the **N** following the **ω** have flaked off the fragment. This kind of defect is not uncommon in ancient papyrus manuscripts. It occurs as a result of incidental abrasions and normal handling.

For example, consider the **K** on the third line of fragment 5 (left leg largely missing), and the space at the end of the fifth line of fragment 1, where we find the word **KOKKINON**. One would think that at least the left leg of the first **N** should appear, but the space on the fragment is completely blank. Similarly, in the John Rylands fragment of the Gospel of John (see Plate XXI), major parts of several letters are extremely faint or completely missing. The **Δ** 's," for instance, on lines 1 and 7 on the front side and the **K** on line 3 of the back side are barely distinguishable. Interestingly enough, C. H. Roberts, the same scholar who dated the Cave 7 fragments, rushed into print in 1934 with his identification of the Rylands fragment, despite the apparent problem letters and variants. The difficulties not withstanding, it became Papyrus 52, and until O'Callaghan's identification of fragment 5 it was the earliest portion of the New Testament ever found.

In summary, it is important to note that in deciphering these problematic letters, O'Callaghan is granted only as much leeway as other experts have been permitted in the past.

A vital point in O'Callaghan's identification of fragment 5 concerns the **KΔI** of line 3. This is a point that several critics pass over in silence. O'Callaghan notes that the **KΔI** is preceded by a space in the fragment. This is in contrast to the fact that fragments 1 through 5 reflect the common practice of running words together. It appears, therefore, that the space

Plate XXI
The John Rylands Fragment, Papyrus 52

is deliberate and indicates the beginning of a new section.

This means that the **ΚΑΙ** is not nearly so common a word as some have thought; it is not "and" but "And" with a capital "A." The space preceding the **ΚΑΙ** indicates that is is not simply an "and" found in a list of two or more items; it is not an "and" in a compound sentence; and it is not even an "And" (capital "A") linking two sentences of the same paragraph. Instead it is the first word of a new section or paragraph, and therefore the **ΚΑΙ** can be expected to play a significant role in the identification of the fragment.

More than this, the **ΚΑΙ** is unique for another reason. Unlike Hebrew, Greek syntax does not usually allow for starting sentences or new paragraphs with "And." In the place of "And" used with whole sentences, Greek requires the use of subordinate clauses. For instance, if Mark 6:52,53 had been written by a native Greek speaker, he would have written, "After they finished the crossing, then they came to Gennessaret where they made fast," rather than, "And they finished the crossing. . . ."

In other words, the particular character of the **ΚΑΙ** on fragment 5 was a hint that the writing might represent "learned" Greek rather than "native" Greek. The writer presumably was born and grew up as a non-Greek and learned Greek as a second language. He wrote Greek words, but his syntax followed his native Semitic tongue.

The conjecture of the original editors of *Discoveries* that the fragment is a biblical text, rather than a text from classical Greek or native Greek, is thus supported by O'Callaghan's astute observation. Many scholarly critics now have suggested alternative identifications from classical (that is pure Greek) texts; however, it is very evident that such alternatives do not match the evidence of fragment 5.

But what about the changes O'Callaghan must assume in the text to explain the peculiar features of the fragment? The critics point to his explanation of **ΤΙ**, "ti" in the third line where all other known manuscripts read **ΔΙ**, "di". They Also balk at the suggestion that three words "to the land" may have been left out in the fourth line preceding *Gennesaret*. These words, if included in the text, tend to make the line too long and destroy the stichometry.

O'Callaghan does not feel that there is an absolute need to omit the phrase. However, there is some evidence that other ancient texts substitute another reading. Even some of the critics have yielded on the inclusion or exclusion of this phrase.

The most important variant required by O'Callaghan is the most difficult. It involves an alteration of the common Greek prepositon **ΔΙΔ**, which is often attached to verbal forms in a similar way as the English "in" in "inborn." In fragment 5, the verbal form *diaperasantes*, which means "finished the crossing" or "having crossed over," appears as *tiaperasantes*. The shift from "d" to "t" is not unknown in papyri from Egypt or other areas where Semitic speaking populations wrote Greek as they heard it rather than as it should have been in proper Greek spelling.

O'Callaghan and others have made a detailed study of the shift in the dental sounds "d" to "t" and the reverse. To quote just one authority, "Bilingual interference in stops begins with the identification of the dental stops "d" and "t" by many writers from the second century B.C. on."[2] Of particular interest in this regard is the famous warning inscription posted at the gate of Herod's temple to restrict entrance to Jews only. The term DRUPHAKTOU, "barrier," is written on the actual stone as TRUPHAKTOU, while in Josephus's historical account it is spelled correctly.

There are numerous other examples that show that this shift from "d" to "t" is not an unusual, much less unique, phenomenon. On all grounds, the identification is as stable as

---

[2]F. T. Gignac, "The Pronunciation of Greek Stops in the Papyri," *Transactions and Proceedings of the American Philological Association*, No. 101, 1970. p. 201.

many others that are the daily standard of papyrologists. Final judgment on the correctness of the identification will only be complete when other fragments of equally early papyri of the New Testament become available for comparison. And that awaits the archaeologist's spade and the papyrologist's decipherment.

Fragment 4

In the fourth issue of volume 53 of *Biblica*, O'Callaghan published identifications of three more of the fragments from Cave 7. The largest and most important was fragment 4 (see Plate XXII). Physically, fragment 4 is even larger than 5, and it represents the right-hand margin of the column. O'Callaghan identified it as 1 Timothy 3:16; 4:1–3.

> . . . believed on in the world, taken up into glory. Now the Spirit speaks expressly, that in the latter times some shall depart from the faith, giving heed to deceitful spirits, and doctrines of devils; speaking lies in hypocrisy; having their conscience seared with a hot iron; Forbidding to marry, and to abstain from meats, which God has created to be. . . .

The following diagram shows *Discoveries'* reading (Column I), O'Callaghan's reading (Column II), modern reconstruction (Column III), and the number of letters per line in "O'Callaghan's reconstruction (Column IV).

As with all of O'Callaghan's identifications, the stichometry, the number of letters per line, works out quite well. Critics have proposed a number of alternative readings for fragment 4. However, none of them yield an acceptable stichometry because all require too much variation in the lengths of the lines. The argument has been presented that ancient texts often vary greatly in the number of letters per line. While this is true of the more cursive, running letter

I	II
]η]των].νται]πνευ]γιμο [..]]οθε	[σινεπιστευθηενκοσμωανεληµφθ]η [ενδοξη τοδεπνευµαρη]των [λεγιωστεροισκαιροισαποστησ]ονται [τινεστησπιστεωπροσεχοντεσ]πνευ [µασινπλανησκαιδιδασκαλιαισδ]ηµο [νιωνενυποκρισειψευδολογωνκε] [καυστηριασµενωντηνιδιανσυνει] [δησινκωλιο]ντ[ωνγαµειναπεχεσθαι] [βρωµατωνα]οθε[οσεκτισενεισµετα]

III	IV
[σιν,ἐπιστεύθη ἐν κόσμῳ ἀνελήμφθ]η	28 letters
[ἐν δόξῃ. Τὸ δὲ πνεῦμα ῥη]τῶν	not applicable
[λέγει 'υστέροις καιροῖς ἀποστήσ]ονταί	31 letters
[τινες τῆς πίστεως, προσέχοντες]πνεύ–	30 letters
[μασιν πλάνης καὶ διδασκαλίαις δ]ημο–	31 letters
[νίων εν ὑποκρίσει ψευδολόγων,·κε–]	27 letters
[καυστηριασμένων τὴν ἰδίαν συνεί–]	28 letters
[δησιν,κωλυό]ντ[ων γαμεῖν,'απέχεσθαι]	29 letters
[βρωμάτων ἅ] ὁ θε[ὸς ἔκτισεν εἰς μετα–]	28 letters

103

Plate XXII
Fragment 4

forms, it is certainly not true of the elaborate *Zierstil* or "decorative" uncial. The reading of fragment 4 has the advantage of being a right-hand margin. In addition to requiring a reasonable stichometry to fill each line to the left margin, the successful decipherment must find a place for the tiny loose scrap listed by the *Discoveries'* editors as part of fragment 4.

O'Callaghan has mentioned that after his identification of fragment 5, he then turned to fragment 4. In this two-part papyrus remnant, it was the letters **ΠΝΕΥ** that first caught his attention. He notes that on only one letter does he differ with the reading of the original editors. In fact, the editors themselves suggested the full word **ΠΝΕΥΜΑ**, the common biblical word for "spirit." Assuming that the distinguished authors and editors had already exhausted all of the possible passages from the Greek Old Testament, the Septuagint, O'Callaghan went right to the New Testament and soon located the two fragments 4₁ and 4₂ in 1 Timothy.

O'Callaghan considers the identifications of fragment 5 as Mark 6:52,53 and fragment 4 as 1 Timothy 3:16, 4:1–3 as the most certain. When asked directly, he said that on a scale of zero to ten in certainty, with zero equalling no certainty and ten equalling one hundred percent certainty, he would place these two identifications at the top with a ten.

Fragment 6

O'Callaghan's next most certain identifications are of fragments 6₁ and 8. However, because of their smaller size and the very apparent probability that a large number of texts could be rearranged to fit the letters on the fragment, the certainty of the identifications obviously is reduced. However, there is the important matter that these tiny fragments reveal grammatical features that are not typical of the Septuagint Old Testament but instead are found in Koiné Greek, the language of the New Testament.

In the same 1972 issue of *Biblica* in which he proposed his identification of fragment 5, O'Callaghan proposed his reading of fragment 6₁ as Mark 4:28 (see Plate XXIII):

> For the earth brings forth fruit of itself; first the blade, then the ear, after that the full grain in the ear.

The following diagram shows *Discoveries'* reading (Column I), O'Callaghan's reading (Column II), modern reconstruction (Column III), number of letters per line in O'Callaghan's reconstruction (Column IV).

I	II
].[	[ηγηκαρπο]φ[ορειπρωτον]
]ειτ..[	[χορτον]ειτεγ[σταχυν]
].ᾰη..[	[ειτεν]πληρη[σιτονεντω]

III	IV
['η γῆ καρπο]φ[ορεῖ, πρῶτον]	19 letters
[χόρτον,]εῖτεγ[στάχυν]	17 letters
[εῖτεν]πλήρη[σῖτον ἐν τῷ]	19 letters

THE EARTH FRUIT BRINGS FORTH FIRST
THE BLADE THEN THE EAR
THEN THE FULL GRAIN IN THE

As with each of the other fragments identified by O'Callaghan, his detractors have debated over whether or not his reconstructions of various letters are correct. In all but a few cases, these critics were working with the poor quality photographs or editor's transcriptions in *Discoveries*. In the

Plate XXIII
Fragment 6

case of fragment 6₁, however, O'Callaghan accepted all of the readings of the original editors. All of his proposed letters appear reasonable on the basis of greatly improved and enlarged photographs, but this the reader may judge. It is interesting to note that this fragment of Mark appears to be from a different papyrus roll, or at least was written by a different hand than fragment 5.

Fragment 8

In the same issue of *Biblica*, O'Callaghan proposed an identification for fragment 8 (see Plate XXIV). He read this four-line fragment as James 1:23,24.

> ". . .or if any be a hearer of the word, and not a doer, he is like one who looks in a mirror at his natural face. He looks and goes away and immediately forgets what sort of man he was.

Again it is necessary to look carefully at the work of the original editors and then at O'Callaghan's proposed identification. Our diagram shows *Discoveries'* reading (Column I), O'Callaghan's reading (Column II), modern reconstruction (Column III), number of letters per line in O'Callaghan's reconstruction (Column IV).

I	II
σ[	σ[ωποντησγενεσεωσαυτουεν]
εσο[	εσο[πτρωκατενοησενκαιαπε]
λη[	λη[λυθενκαιευθεωσεπελαθε]
ν[	

III	IV
σ[ωπον τῆς γενέσεως αὐτοῦ ἐν]	23 letters
ἐσο[πτρῳ· κατενόησεν καὶ ἀπε]	23 letters
λή[λυθεν καὶ εὐθέως ἐπελάθε]	23 letters

... HIS NATURAL IN A
MIRROR. HE LOOKS AND GO
ES AWAY AND IMMEDIATELY FOR

O'Callaghan feels the possible **N** which the editors proposed for the fourth line is problematic at best:

> The **N** is incomplete and due to another hand, and is not only more distant from the last line than the lines are from each other (distance of 8mm from line 3, while only 4mm separate line 2 from 3), but it also leaves a distance of some 4mm from the margin. This alone suggests that it does not belong to the preceding text. It is, consequently, somewhat superfluous, a letter whose specific function is quite difficult to decide, given what little of the rest is preserved. Could it not be a letter written in the lower margin as an aid to the calculation of the lines of writing (Stichoe) which would usually be noted down at the end of the columns along with the title of the book?

The fragments from Cave 7, then, provide us with both examples of the upper-right corner of a column in fragment 7 and with the lower-left corner of another column in fragment 8. One fact is clear from the examination of these two corner

Plate XXIV
Fragments 8 and 9

fragments that show opposite left and right margins: the columns of letters are even and neatly in line. This means that the numbers of letters per line can be identified within narrow limits. This is the single aspect of O'Callaghan's careful effort that is overlooked by would-be critics who feel they have found alternative passages that will satisfy the requirements of the fragments. As small as the fragments are and as scant the writing, the real elegance of O'Callaghan's identifications is that they fit the passages and the line lengths and at the same time retain virtually every certain letter of the original editors who had no idea what these fragments represent.

Fragment 6₂

In the July/December 1972 segment of *Studia Papyrologica*, O'Callaghan published three more detailed studies on his identifications. These were of fragments 6₂, 7, and 9. He identified the first small fragment as Acts 27:38 (see Plate XXII):

. . . seventy six. When they had eaten as much as they wanted they lightened the ship by dumping the grain into the sea.

The chart below shows *Discoveries'* reading (Column I), O'Callaghan's reading (Column II), modern reconstruction (Column III), number of letters per line in O'Callaghan's reconstruction (Column IV).

I	II	
]τορ[ ]ουφ.[	[δομηκονταεξ]κορ[εσθεντεσ] [δετροφησεκ]ουφι[ζοντοπλοι]	
	III	IV
	[δομήκοντα ἕξ.] κορ[εσθέντες] [δὲ τροφης ἐκ]ουφι[ζον τὸ πλοι–]	23 letters 23 letters

111

ENTY SIX EAT N WHEN THEY HAD ENOUGH FOODTHEYLIGHTENED THE SHIP

O'Callaghan's clue to the identification of fragment 62 was the rather rare combination of letters **ΟΥΦ**, which appears only very occasionally in the New Testament. In fact, the verb "to lighten" is what is termed a *hapax legémenon,* that is, a word occurring only once in the New Testament text. It is interesting that the critics of O'Callaghan's proposals have had little success with this fragment. The handwriting of the fragment is a particularly florid *Zierstil* style and its significance will be discussed in the next chapter.

Fragment 7

The second fragment identified in the *Studia Papyrologica* article was fragment 7 (see Plate XXV). While the traces are difficult, they are extremely interesting and offer one of the most fascinating possibilities of all the fragments.

The special excitement is that the top line, though very fragmentary, appears to contain traces of the name "Jesus." O'Callaghan identifies the fragment as the very familiar Mark 12:17:

> Jesus said to them, 'Render to Caesar the things that are Caesar's, and to God the things that are God's.' And they wondered at him.

Ten years ago Rabbi Samuel Sandmel of Hebrew Union College, Jewish Institute of Religion, addressed the Society of

Plate XXV
Fragment 7

113

Biblical Literature and Exegesis and asserted that the Dead Sea Scrolls would be far more exciting if only they mentioned known people and events. "I would gladly swap all the sectarian documents and hymns for one tiny Qumran fragment that would contain the name of Jesus or Caiaphas or James or Paul," exclaimed Sandmel.

Fragment 7 appears to do exactly that by containing both the name Jesus and the title Caesar. Let us again compare the reading O'Callaghan supposes with the work of the original editors. The diagram shows: *Discoveries'* reading (Column I); O'Callaghan's reading (Column II; the modern reconstruction (Column III) and the number of letters per line in O'Callaghan's reconstruction (Column IV). It must be noted here that ancient documents often have special abbreviations for sacred names and other frequent titles. O'Callaghan happens to be a recognized authority on such abbreviations and his book on the subject, *Nomina sacra in papyris graecis saeculi III neotestamentariis* (Sacred names in third century Greek papyri of the New Testament) published in 1970, is a standard work used by other papyrologists. The letters believed to be deleted in the abbreviations of "Jesus" and "Caesar" are placed in parenthesis on the chart.

I	II
	[καισαροσ οδεισειπεν]
].[	[αυτ]ο̣[ιστακαισαροσαποδο]
]κ̄α.[	[τε]και[σαριτατουθυτωθωκαιε]
]θα.[	[ξε]θαυ[μαζονεπαυτωκαιερ]

III	IV
[Καίσαρος. ὁ δὲ Ἰ(ησοῦ)ς εἶπεν]	18 letters
[αὐτ]ο̣ῖς, Τὰ Καίσαρος ἀπόδο–]	21 letters
[τε]Καί[σαρί, τὰ τοῦ θ(εο)ῦ τῷ θ(εο)ῷ.Καὶ ἐ–]	24 letters
[ξε] θαύ[μαζον 'επ' αυτῷ Και 'ερ–]	21 letters

The special excitement of this fragment is found partly in the horizontal line over the **K**. The editors of *Discoveries*

TO THEM WHAT IS CAESAR'S RENDER
TO CAESAR WHAT IS GOD'S TO GOD AND TH-
EY WONDERED AT HIM AND

interpret it as an indication of an abbreviated word, for that is how shortened words were marked by ancient scribes. But the enlarged photo reveals that a vertical line starts up from it. In light of this, it seems that we have not a simple horizontal line but the base of a large initial **I**, the first letter of the Greek form of "Jesus."

"Jesus," that is, **IHCOYC**, may actually have appeared in the fragment abbreviated to **IHC** or **IC**, since the sacred names were commonly abbreviated by ancient scribes. However, we cannot be sure of this in the case of first-century and early second-century manuscripts. "Jesus" was apparently not abbreviated in the Rylands fragment identified by Roberts.

Another name, or at least title, that appears in fragment 7 is "Caesar" (line 2); we see the **KA** of KAISAR, the Greek spelling. The identification of fragment 7, then, seems very promising. And again, O'Callaghan's work is based on exact agreement with the transcription of the original editors (except for the interpretation of the horizontal line). The very fact that we may have here a fragment of one of the best known passages from the Gospels adds to the excitement. Needless to say, the tiny scrap with only its suggestion of seven letters is classed by O'Callaghan as a "probable" and most assuredly not a "certain" identification.

While the fragment is small, the horizontal line near the top

115

of the **K** is of great importance. The verbal form **EΞEΘAYMAZON** is not overly common and along with the initial **KAI** of Caesar adds great weight to O'Callaghan's proposal. These two words occur together in the New Testament only in the suggested passage, Mark 12:17.

Fragment 9

The last fragment discussed in the *Studia Papyrologica* article was number 9, which was identified as a portion of Romans 5:11,12 (see Plate XXIV):

> . . . but we also joy in God through our Lord Jesus Christ, by
> whom we have now received the atonement. Wherefore, as by
> one man sin entered into the world, and death by sin; and so
> death passed upon all men, for that all have sinned.

Again, the chart gives us *Discoveries'* reading (Column I), O'Callaghan's reading (Column II), the modern reconstruction (Column III), and the number of letters per line in O'Callaghan's reconstruction (Column IV).

I]αγην]]...[	II [νυντηνκαταλλ]αγην[ελαβο] [μεν διατουτο]ωσπ[ερδιενοσ]		
	III [νῦν τὴν καταλλ]αγὴν['ελάβο–] [μεν. Δὶα τοῦτο] ὤσπ[ερ δι 'ένὸς]	IV 21 letters 22 letters	

Whether or not O'Callaghan is right hinges on the proper transcription of the incomplete letters of the second line. Ordinarily, the top portion of such a group of letters would be quite sufficient to suggest one or more plausible transcriptions. But in this case what appears is rather puzzling. While the whole letters on the top line seem to

RECONCILIATION WE RECEI VED WHEREFORE AS BY ONE

reflect a more or less standard uncial style, this hardly seems the case with the remnants of line 2. In some respects they verge on the character of first-century cursive Greek rather than uncial. But given the meager evidence, O'Callaghan's identification seems plausible until an in depth study can be made of the fragment and proposed possible alternatives can be examined.

Fragment 10

In 1974, two years after his first announcement, O'Callaghan put all of his studies on the fragments and answers to certain specific criticisms into book form: *Los Papiros Griegos de la Cueva 7 de Qumran*, published by Biblioteca de Autores Cristianos. Along with the seven fragments already detailed, O'Callaghan gave details on two or more identifications he considered "possible" but with very low degrees of certainty. These were fragments 10 and 15.

Fragment 10 was identified as a portion of 2 Peter 1:15;

be able after my death to have these things always in remembrance.

In the chart we have *Discoveries'* reading (Column I), O'Callaghan's reading (Column II), modern reconstruction (Column III), and the number of letters in the lines of O'Callaghan's reconstruction (Column IV).

I	II	
].[ ]..νε.[	[δασωδεκαιεκαστο]τ̣[εεχειν] [υμασμετατηνε]μηνεξ[οδον]	

III	IV
[δάσω δὲ καὶ 'εκάστο]τ[ε 'εχειν] ['υμᾶς μετὰ τὴν 'ε]μὴν ἔξ[οδον]	22 letters 21 letters

EAGER ALWAYS TO HAVE
AFTER MY DEATH

Regarding fragment 10, the original editors are certain only of the **Є**. They suggest **N** for the following letter and O'Callaghan agrees. In a footnote they conjecture that the preceding letter may be **Π**. The context of O'Callaghan's suggested identification, however, demands an **M** at this point. With the advantage of our greatly enlarged photo (see Plate XXVI) there is little difficulty seeing the plausibility of this preference. Many admit that this reading fits the evidence as well as any.

Fragment 15

The last identification presented is fragment 15, which appears to be another portion of Mark. O'Callaghan locates it as Mark 6:48:

Plate XXVI
Fragments 10 and 15

. . . seeing them striving to now for the wind was against
them. . . .

We will again compare the readings of the original editors
with O'Callaghan's proposals: *Discoveries'* reading
(Column I); O'Callaghan's reading (Column II); modern
reconstruction (Column III), and the number of letters in the
lines of O'Callaghan's reconstruction (Column IV).

I ἐ]ν τῷ ε.[ ]....[	II [νουσε]ντωιελ[αυνεινηνγαρ] [οανεμο]σε[ν]α[ντιοσαυτοισ]·	
	III [νους ἐ]ν τῷ ἐλ[αύνειν, ἤν γὰρ] [ὁ ἄνεμο]ς᾿ε[ν]ἁ[ντιος αὐτοῖς]	IV 22 letters 21 letters

STRIVING TO ROW FOR
THE WIND WAS AGAINST THEM

This is from the same chapter of Mark as fragment 5, but the
two are from different scribal hands. Fragment 6₁ is also from
Mark but does not appear to be a part of the same papyri as
either 5 or 15. But this is not at all strange. If it seems strange
that Cave 7 should yield four copies of Mark, it must be
remembered that Cave 7 also yielded fragments from 14
different copies of Deuteronomy, and more than two dozen
fragments of different copies of Isaiah have been recovered at
Qumran.

Summary

It only remains to be said that O'Callaghan's identification of any one fragment from Cave 7 gains credibility by the fact that he was able to establish New Testament identifications of the other fragments as well.

Consider, for instance, the doubtfulness of the identifications if all of the fragments except one or two had already been identified with the Old Testament and various writings of the Qumran sect. Then a claim to have made the revolutionary discovery that fragment 5 was from the New Testament would seem highly improbable. To be sure, anything is possible, and so such a claim would rank as a "possible" identification even in isolation. But it would seem rather inexplicable for a lone New Testament text to be found among such a collection. The isolation would make it many times more difficult to accept than O'Callaghan's findings. His nine identifications tremendously reinforce one another. He can even afford to be wrong on two or three of them without suffering a serious threat to the basic thrust of his work.

It also is most impressive that out of a total of seventy-three "certain" and "uncertain" letters transcribed by the original editors, O'Callaghan agrees with them on sixty-five. That is a remarkable record, considering the fragmentary and indistinct condition of some of the "uncertain" letters. And equal in importance to this is the matter of the dating of the fragments from Cave 7.

Dating of the Fragments

The original dating came from C. H. Roberts, who expressed himself in a letter to one of the principal editors of the *Discoveries* series, the late Roland de Vaux. His opinion was so valued by the editors of volume III that it was cited as authoritative.

Roberts's date for fragment 5 was 50 B.C. to A.D. 50. To bracket the fragment or manuscript within the limits of a century or half-century is the most acceptable way to date on paleographic grounds. Perhaps in this connection it would be illuminating to interject Roberts's own work with the Rylands fragment of the Gospel of John. When he announced his discovery, he settled for the first half of the second century as the approximate date of the fragment. He arrived at this by noting that the scribal hand most closely resembled a manuscript firmly dated at A.D. 95, and that it was also similar, but less so, to a manuscript dated about A.D. 150. On this basis, one often finds A.D. 125–135 given as the approximate date of the Rylands fragment.

A further matter of interest is that scholars have reasoned that since the Rylands fragment was found in Egypt (a good distance from Ephesus in Asia Minor where it is thought that John wrote his Gospel), up to a full generation of about thirty years could be allowed between the time that John wrote and the time that the Egyptian scribe was able to produce his copy. In other words, Roberts's discovery was the first firm archaeological evidence that the Gospel of John was written about the end of the first century and not in the middle of the second century as a number of liberal scholars and negative higher critics had maintained.

The matter of the dating is inseparable from the circumstances of the discovery of Cave 7 and the paleography, that is, the style of writing. There are three important points to be maintained here.

1. The archaeologists who discovered and excavated Cave 7 are said to have put the sealing of the cave at no later than A.D. 70. This then would be the date beyond which nothing in the cave could be dated. Therefore, the attempt by some critics to stretch the dating of some of the fragments to A.D. 200 to 150 is impossible.

2. The editors of *Discoveries* themselves noted that fragment 1 (Exod. 28:4–7) was written in "rounded writing with small curves decorating the ends of certain characters, and which Schubart calls the *Zierstil*. They apply the same term to fragments 3–5: ". . . the writing belongs to *Zierstil* and could date to 50 B.C. or A.D. 50." So it is clear that the *Zierstil* character of the fragments is worth investigating.

Indeed, O'Callaghan pursues the subtle differences in the *Zierstil* even further and notes that fragments 6₁ and 8 are similar to a grouping of such papyri that were found at the ruins of the Roman town Herculaneum. This city on the Bay of Naples was destroyed and completely burned along with its sister city, Pompei, in August of A.D. 79 by the eruption of Vesuvius. During the eighteenth century various excavators turned up a large collection of papyrus scrolls carbonized by the lava and ash. These are the only papyri ever recovered from Roman-Age Italy. They are mostly the teachings of Epicurean philosophers of the Roman Empire. Many of the works are in Greek and in a unique decorative uncial style. It has been pointed out that most of the books of the New Testament from which O'Callaghan has identified the fragments—Mark, 1 Timothy, 2 Peter, and Romans—are all associated by tradition with Rome. Then there is also the large jar with the name "Rome" written in Hebrew letters. This all points to an Italian origin for the papyri.

The conclusion is simple: These fragments from the tiny cave on the Northwest shore of the Dead Sea are evidence of manuscripts written in fine scribal hands and used by the wealthiest Roman literati (for only the rich could afford hand-copied manuscripts) in the heart of Italy before A.D. 79.

3. Most amazing of all is the fact that the fragments do not represent autographs, that is, original compositions of the books. All the flourishes used by professional copyists are seen in the fragments—the uncial *Zierstil* style and the even lines

and justified margins proven by fragments 4 and 8.

The uncial style was seldom used for original writing but was reserved for the use of scribes who were preserving manuscripts that had come to be recognized as important literature. A modern analogy would be that a typewritten manuscript could conceivably be the author's original, but a typeset, printed copy would certainly not be the author's original.

The copies represented by the fragments were the published form of the original books. The early dates become even more startling because they mean that within the lifetimes of the apostles and their associates who wrote the books, they were copied by scribes, the ancient equivalent of publication, and distributed.

These three important points demand certain conclusions for the proper understanding of the origins of the New Testament. But what are those conclusions and what do they mean for the careful student of the Holy Scriptures and others who seek to honor the Scriptures and take them seriously?

8
Proof and Disproof

A WORD of caution must be stated here. The material evidence from Cave 7 is so small that the very best deductions are, and will always be, carefully weighed guesses. O'Callaghan and others have frequently pointed out that many classical and nonliterary papyri have been identified with less evidence than those of Cave 7. However, equal caution must be directed toward those who would hide behind a facade of academic objectivity but who simply seek acceptance by the majority and preferment from their peers. As one contemporary writer once commented, "The implications of such an identification are such that I suppose it was inevitable that much of the reaction should be partisan. But the lack of objectivity and restraint on the part of some scholars can only be construed as bad manners, at best."[1] As the years since 1972 have passed, no alternative has been agreed upon as the solution to the mysterious tiny scraps of papyri.

[1]Wilbur N. Pickering, *The Identity of the New Testament Text* (Nashville: Thomas Nelson, 1977), see appendix.

Six Requirements

In an article supporting the identifications published in early 1973, one of the present authors listed the six requirements that were met by O'Callaghan's proposals but remained to be satisfied on all grounds by the frequently proposed alternatives.

1. *The text must exist.* One of the spectacular features of O'Callaghan's discovery is that the identifications were made in a body of texts well known to millions of human beings, the New Testament. There was no necessity whatsoever for any redaction, emendation, or translation of the material into another language in which no version of the text is known to exist. The pure fact is that any proposed text that must be deduced from the reading of one version and then translated into the linguistic system of another will always be an artifact. Some of the seemingly best alternatives that have been proposed require a retranslation of the text into the Hebrew since they don't represent any known version of the Greek Old Testament.

2. *The lines must fit a known stichometry* (the number of letters in each line). In all cases, O'Callaghan's texts can be arranged to fit the stichometry of the line without ingenuity; however, some assumptions are involved and must be examined in detail. The problem with many of the proposed alternatives is that they require very irregular line lengths of sixty-five characters followed by forty followed by twenty-five. These are unusual cases and do not fit nearly as well as O'Callaghan's proposed readings.

3. *Lines must break regularly.* Ancient texts do not just break lines wherever they happen to fall by letter count. Even though the words are run together, the lines usually end with the ends of words. This prinicple has been followed by all

lower critics of Greek and Latin manuscripts going back to Petrarch in the early Renaissance. The overwhelming majority of split words are divided at the break in syllables, dipthongs, or consonant clusters; initial phonemes are very rarely divided. Therefore a goodly number of the proposed identifications that have been circulated can be dismissed out of hand. There may be texts that have uneven breaks, but these are definitely the exceptions to the rule.

4. *The orthography (spelling and transcription) must be internally consistent.* Although so-called mixed texts, those exhibiting aspects of two different orthographic systems, do exist, they are consistent in transliterating the same sounds in the same fashion. Too often, scholars supply unknowns or obscurities to form an emendation, a change, in a known context. The two most outrageous examples of this are the use of the obscure Greek dialects to find koiné lexical units, a practice that died in the last years of the nineteenth century, and the still unacceptable habit of many Old Testament commentators of picking roots from the Arabic dictionaries to solve problems in the Old Testament. All of the Qumran 7 fragments are uniform in being written in the *Zierstil* or decorative style. They are also clearly on scrolls while no other Christian text of such antiquity or of such a format has been recovered.

5. *The text must be consistent with the location.* Cave 7 is in a very desolate part of the Middle East, not a place given to either frequent commerce or travel at any time in history. For this reason the context proposed as an alternative must be one that was known in Judea in the first two Christian centuries, acceptable to the people of the north shore of the Dead Sea during the period, and worthy of being stored away in a system of caves widely known to be used for the storage of sacred Jewish books. The obvious fact, therefore, is that these

fragments are also religious in nature. The primary religious text of the Roman Imperial Period was the New Testament.

6. *A body of material must be proposed.* Only one fragment, fragment 1, can be positively identified as coming from the Greek Old Testament, the Septuagint, and even then extensive alterations must be made in the standard text of the Septuagint to make it fit. Not one of the three other longest fragments, fragment 3, fragment 7, and fragment 18, has been located in the Septuagint. Fragment 2, identified as a portion of the Pseudepigrapha cannot in anyway be counted as a part of the Old Testament in either Hebrew or Greek. To propose a text totally apart from the religious literature so far discovered may cause some doubt on a particular text identification but can never solve the overall problem of the collection.[2]

Subjective Considerations

However, through both 1972 and 1973, the detractors increased their dissent. But it must be noted that unlike most scholarly discoveries, the identifications of the Cave 7 fragments had enormous political and religious ramifications. Not surprisingly, David Flusser, an Israeli scholar of the Dead Sea Scrolls, summed up the attitude of his colleagues in the Department of Antiquities when he branded the proposal, "fanciful and wild speculation."

It is important to keep in mind that there are nonscholarly, subjective aspects to the whole controversy:

1. It has only been five years since O'Callaghan's original proposal, and it is not unusual for confirmation in such highly technical matters to require from a decade to a whole

[2]William White, Jr., "Notes on the Papyrus Fragments from Cave 7 at Qumran," *The Westminster Theological Journal*, Vol. 35, No. 2, Winter 1973.

generation to appear. At the time of this writing, new points of view from scholars not originally involved with the affair are apparently leaning toward O'Callaghan's identifications.

2. Most of the original dissent involved three aspects. First, there is no clear connection between the Qumran community and the New Testament. O'Callaghan never claimed there was; however, that the very location of Cave 7 is a good distance closer to Jericho has been utterly ignored by these critics. Second, they have unanimously focused on fragment 5 without regard to either fragment 4, which is certainly the right-hand margin of a page, or the intriguing reverse image in the soil, imprint 1, which includes a phrase found nowhere in the Old Testament and universally recognized as of Christian origin. Third, many, many subjective factors intrude on the best-intentioned efforts in regard to the fragments. Above all the controversy pits Israeli experts, who are not overly experienced with New Testament papyri, against a specialist in the early history of Christianity. Furthermore, it plays Catholic Dominicans in Jerusalem against a Jesuit in Barcelona; Frenchmen and Englishmen against a Spaniard; liberal views of the New Testament against a discovery that could go far to pull the rug out from under accepted liberal theological assumptions; the work of a newcomer to the Dead Sea Scrolls (O'Callaghan) against the works of long-established experts who were responsible for the authoritative work on the subject.

These remarks are not intended to be impertinent or argumentative. They are simply a candid recognition of human factors that can complicate the picture. The present authors readily acknowledge that they are not free from such presuppositions, and wise readers will take into account their conservative commitments.

We are not, however, the first to raise the question of subjective influences. Joseph A. Fitzmyer, writing dispassionately in the Jesuit journal *America*, noted that Baillet, editor of *Discoveries*, "thinks that O'Callaghan is all wrong. But could this be the original editor's reluctance to admit that someone else has succeeded where he did not?" And, in commenting on Roberts's dissent: ". . . is it a case of a Spaniard succeeding where an Englishman failed?"[3]

Numerical Odds

We have explained the six requirements that were met by O'Callaghan's proposals and discussed the subjective considerations that should be taken into account in analyzing the objections to his work. However, the most formidable evidence of the validity of his discovery is the numerical odds that he is right.

Using just the letters identified in the same way by both O'Callaghan and the editors of *Discoveries*, we can make up what is called a "character string" consisting of the following probabilities.

Kappa Alpha Iota (**KΑΙ**) occurs 1 time in 20 in Greek manuscripts. that is, out of any 20 words picked at random, 1 will be **KΑΙ**.

Kappa Alpha Iota plus Tau Omega (**KΑΙΤѠ**) occurs 1 time out of every 10 times that **KΑΙ** occurs.

Kappa Alpha Iota Tau Omega plus one additional unidentified letter occurs 1 time out of every 50 times that **KΑΙΤѠ** occurs.

So the odds on just this five character string plus one more unidentified character is 1 in 10,000. And if we take the line

---

[3]"A Qumran Fragment of Mark?" *America*, June 24, 1972, p. 649.

out to nine characters plus one further unidentified letter, the odds climb to 1 in 30,000,000. New Testament computer-studies expert A. Q. Morton of Edinburg, Scotland, has stated that there are only about 11,250 words in all of Mark or 56,250 characters, vastly less by a factor of 1,000 than the odds for just one character string. When one figures in the strings from all the identifications that number more than fifty characters, the odds of locating the total identification in some other source jumps to something above 2.25×10^{65}, which is the number 2.25 multiplied by 10 and followed by 65 zeros!

9
What Do the Fragments from Cave 7 Mean?

FOR SCHOLARS, the Cave 7 fragments mean that the earliest Christian writings were written on scrolls and copied by scribes in the best Roman fashion of the first century. They mean that new investigations should be carried on to locate more New Testament material, not only among the Dead Sea Scrolls but also among other first-century material written in the *Zierstil* style. When one realizes that only a small portion of the ancient city Herculaneum near Pompeii has yet been excavated, the potential discoveries overwhelm the mind—might there still be part of the Book of Romans or 2 Peter still lying entombed in the mud and ash from that fateful summer day in A.D. 79?

For the Bible student, the meaning is wide ranging. Firstly, the tiny scraps mean that Christian attempts to set down and record the events of Jesus' ministry began so near the time of Christ—if not during His ministry itself—that there was just no time for the development of myths and legends and the complex literary phenomena required by the theories of liberal critics such as Rudolph Bultmann.

A century ago, one of the founders of negative higher criticism and innovators of the "quest for the historical Jesus," D. F. Strauss, put his views this way:

It would most unquestioningly be an argument of decisive weight in favor of the credibility of the biblical history, could it indeed be shown that it was written by eye-witnesses, or even by persons nearly contemporaneous with the events narrated. [1]

Strauss has been followed by legions of unbelieving scholars who totally doubted that any evidence would ever come to the fore that would show that the writers of the New Testament were indeed eyewitnesses of the events they recorded.

Now, however, the tiny fragments raise the edge of the curtain of history and reveal an earlier date for the writing and collection of the New Testament than ever thought possible. The Hegelian disputes within the early church, which are so much a part of modern reconstructions of apostolic history, evaporate in the cold, hard light of evidence.

In summarizing the powerful modern school of thought initiated by Bultmann, N. B. Stonehouse, late Professor of New Testament at Westminster Theological Seminary, wrote,

In its effort to recover the primary stratum of the gospel tradition, this method proceeds in three distinct stages—a preliminary stage in which the stories and sayings are isolated from their contexts in the Gospels, a second in which the isolated units are subjected to internal criticism with a view to the recovery of their supposed original form in oral tradition, and a final stage in which, through this application of external criticism, units that supposedly reflect situations that arose after the death of Jesus are eliminated as anchronistic. Those that remain after this process of reduction and elimination are received as authentic witnesses to the purpose of Jesus. [2]

[1] *The Life of Jesus*, critically examined; translated from the 4th German ed. Vol 1 (London: Chapman, 1846) p. 88.
[2] *Paul Before the Areopagus* (Grand Rapids, Mich.: Wm. B. Eerdmans, 1957) p. 123.

Plate XXVII
Street scenes of Pompei as it was in A.D. 79. The city was rediscovered in 1748.

Bultmann himself wrote,

> I do indeed think that we can now know almost nothing concerning the life and personality of Jesus, since the early Christian sources show no interest in either, are moreover fragmentary and often legendary; and other sources about Jesus do not exist.[3]

Unfortunately, the great German scholar did not live long enough to see his lifework of criticism undone by the tiny papyri from Qumran, but its epitaph could not have been better stated than by an anonymous scholar quoted by *Time* magazine who said of O'Callaghan's discoveries: "They can make a bonfire of 70 tons of indigestible German scholarship."

It would be encouraging if such frank realization would dawn upon the world of religious scholarship, and a revival of faith in the truth of the Gospels would result. However, historical precedent would indicate that this optimistic expectation will not be satisfied. It behooves the laymen and women who sit in the pews and pay the bills to demand that their clergy and denominational professors give the date and authority of the New Testament a new and reverent consideration.

When the original flurry of excitement over O'Callaghan's discovery was at its peak, one of the present authors stated, "If this leading papyrologist is correct, all contemporary Barthian and Bultmannian views of the New Testament's formation will come crashing down in one inglorious heap."[4] As strange as it may seem, a number of scholars could not see this point and seemed stunned and even hurt that the towering figure of contemporary theology could have been wrong. After all, wasn't Barth a theologian and not a New Testament scholar?

---

[3]"Jesus and the Word," English Translation, *Scribners*, 1958, p. 8.
[4]William White, Jr., "A Laymen's Guide to O'Callaghan's Discovery," *Eternity*, June 1972, p. 29.

But what such devotees are overlooking is the fact that Barth openly acknowledged that his "Church Dogmatics" began where the critical scholars left off. He thought, as did the German critical scholars before him, that the early church was the true constructor of Christian truth, and his idea of the inspiration of the Gospels as God-breathed narratives was so enshrouded in layers and disputes of German romantic philosophy that it became meaningless. As an article in *Eternity* stated, "The end result of such unrestrained reconstructions is that the modern reader is left with a set of ethical ideals floating in a sea of myth and garbled saga. It is no wonder that the typical college graduate today does not feel he can turn to the New Testament for an authentic record of what Jesus and His disciples really said and did."

But the full ramifications of O'Callaghan's identifications were clear enough to many writers. United Press International columnist Louis Cassels wrote on April 17, 1972,

> Mark's record [therefore] had to survive the acid test of any journalistic or historical writing—being published at a time when it could be read and criticized, and if inauthentic, denounced by thousands of Jews, Christians, Romans and Greeks who were living in Palestine at the time of Jesus' ministry. That the early church chose Mark as one of only four gospels out of dozens once in circulation to be preserved for posterity in the New Testament also indicates the people closest to the events—Jesus' original followers—found Mark's report accurate and trustworthy, not myth but true history.

The fact that O'Callaghan located so many different New Testament books among the fragments is truly remarkable. Among them are books the liberal theologians have widely considered to be fraudulent and not part of the original New Testament or written by their professed authors. The following table shows the books included.

137

Citation	Fragment	Date
Mark 4:28	7Q6$_1$	A.D. 50
Mark 6:48	7Q15	A.D. ?
Mark 6:52,53	7Q5	A.D. 50
Mark 12:17	7Q7	A.D. 50
Acts 27:38	7Q6$_2$	A.D. 60
Romans 5:11,12	7Q9	A.D. 60
1 Timothy 3:16, 4:1–3	7Q4	A.D. 70 +
2 Peter 1:15	7Q10	A.D. 70 +
James 1:23,24	7Q8	A.D. 70 +

Among the fragmentary texts are some of the most important for Christian faith and life. In addition all types of contexts are represented: doctrine, discourse, description, and admonition—the very mixture stated to be impossible at so early a date by many critics. But how did this collection get into the tiny cave?

Inescapable Conclusions

At present we can only surmise that someone from the Christian community at Jericho or the environs hid the jar with its precious contents before the final onslaught of Titus against Jerusalem or during the siege that followed. If O'Callaghan's identifications are correct as we have presented them, then the following conclusions are inescapable:

The Gospel narratives constitute authentic evidence that the words and works of Jesus were recorded and widely known throughout first-century Palestine. The events of the Gospels were openly witnessed and were committed to writing while both the participants and observers still lived. The location of the Cave 7 fragments in a region some distance from Galilee, with five of them dated a decade before the destruction of the temple, would bear this out.

The traditional view that the New Testament is a self-contained collection, a canon, is vindicated. The proximity of so many fragments from so many distant authors, some even being in Rome, bolsters the view that the collection of the New Testament was well under way within the lifetimes of the authors. Peter's mention of Paul in 2 Peter 3:15 lends support to this contention.

The Gospel of Mark, traditionally thought to represent the reminiscences and sermons of Peter, was written down as a continuous narrative at such an early date that the original must have been written before the other Gospels and soon after, if not during, the public ministry of Jesus. It was not under any circumstances, the product of long evolutionary, combinatory, or redactive processes that were dependent upon some supposedly primitive, long-lost source, either oral or literary.

The teachings of the apostles and early disciples were set down in writing with specific regard to the quality of the text and were accorded the same treatment as the most valuable literary works of the time. They were almost immediately copied by learned scribes and distributed widely. They were known and valued during the age of the apostles.

Many of the descriptive, connective, and introductory features found in the New Testament narratives were not literary innovations or stylistic additions of later hands but are original to the text.

It is essentially correct to say that the straightforward message of the New Testament, as transmitted by the majority text through many scribes and many generations, is faithfully represented in today's standard version.

All critical theories and radical reconstructions of apostolic history and the origins of the New Testament must be called into question and held suspect, if not rejected outright.

The believer in the doctrines of historic Christianity and in the message of salvation that calls men of all ages to faith in the

Lord Jesus Christ can only wonder at God's providence in preserving upon one tiny scrap of ancient papyrus the traces of the words of Paul, which sum up forever the Christian's triumph: ". . . we shall also joy in God through our Lord Jesus, through whom we have now been granted reconciliation" (Rom. 5:11).

The First New Testament?

But do these fragments represent portions of the first New Testament? The following facts can help you draw your own conclusion.

The fragments from Qumran Cave 7 are the remains of scrolls. It is well established that the use of the codex, or book with pages, was popularized by Christians and certainly was dominant by the first half of the second century if not earlier.

The books represented by the fragments are the earlier books of the New Testament, yet all three sections of the developing New Testament are represented—the Gospel of Mark, the historical segment of Acts, and Epistles to the Romans, 1 Timothy and 2 Peter. But Paul's epistles to the churches of Asia Minor, Ephesus, Corinth, and Galatia were not found; neither were any of the writings of John, which have been traditionally dated at the last decade of the first and first decade of the second century.

The scrolls were written in a style that at that time, A.D. 50–70, was already past its prime, but a scribal "published" style nonetheless, showing they were circulated.

The "published" New Testament of the generation that arose after the destruction of the temple and the Roman conquest in A.D. 70–73, apparently included all of the books listed by the early church fathers and which we now know.

Here at Qumran then do we not have a glimpse of the Canon of the early church—and thus the first New Testament?

Bibliography

Baillet, M. "Les manuscrits de la grotte 7 de Qumran et le Nouveau Testament." *Biblica*, Rome, 53, 1972, pp. 508–516.

Bartina, S. "Identificación de papiros neotestamentarios en la cueva 7 de Qumrân." *Cultura Biblica*, Segovia, 29, 1972, pp. 195–206.

_____, "Los papiros de la Cueva Sétima de Qumrán: juicios, lecturas, atribuciones y exploración de los ordenadores," *Cultura Biblica*, 32, 1975, pp. 83–105.

Benoit, P. "Note sur les fragments grecs de la grotte 7 de Qumran." *Revue Biblique*, Paris, 79, 1972, pp. 321–324.

Bernardi, J. "L'Évangile de Saint Marc et la grotte 7 de Qumrân." *Etudes Théologiques et Religieuses*, Montpellier, 47, 1972, pp. 453–456.

Briend, J. "La grotte 7 de Qumrân et le Nouveau Testament." *Bible et Terre Sainte*, Paris, 143, 1972, p. 24.

Estrada, D. M. "O'Callaghan's Identifications." *Eternity*, June 1972, p. 26 ff.

_____, "On the Latest Identifications of New Testament Documents." *The Westminster Theological Journal*, 34, No. 1, Spring, 1972, pp. 109–117.

Fitzmyer, F.A. "A Qumran Fragment of Mark?" *America*, June 24, 1972, pp. 647–650.

Fisher, E. "New Testament Documents Among the Dead Sea Scrolls?" *The Bible Today*, Collegeville, Minnesota, 61, 1972, pp. 835–841.

Garnet, P. "O'Callaghan's Fragments: Our Earliest New Testament Texts?" *Evangelical Quarterly*, 45, 1972, pp. 6–12.

Ghiberti, G. "Dobbiamo anticipare la data di composizione dei Vangeli?" *Parole di Vita*, Torino, 17, 1972, pp. 303–306.

Hemer, C.J. "New Testament Fragments at Qumran?" Tyndale Bulletin, Cambridge, 23, 1972, pp. 125–128.

Legrand, L. "The New Testament at Qumran?" *Indian Ecclesiastical Studies*, 11, 1972, pp. 157–166.

Martini, C.M. "Note sui papiri della grotta 7 di Qumrân." *Biblica*, Rome, 53, 1972, pp. 101–104.

_____, "Testi neotestamentari tra i manoscritti del deserto di Giuda?" *La Civiltà Cattolica*, Rome, 123, 1972, pp. 156–158.

Mejía, J. "Un problema biblico; La antigüedaddel Nuevo Testamento." Criterio, Buenos Aires, 45, 1972, pp. 270–273.

Müller, W. "Notas y comentarios, Über PBerl. Inv. 17076," *Studia Papyrologica*, 15, 1976, p. 151.

O'Callaghan, J. *Cartas Cristianas Griegas Del Siglo V*. Editorial Balmes, Barcelona, 1963, (Biblioteca) Histórica de la Biblioteca Balmes, Series 2, Vol. 25.

_____, "¿I Tim. 3:16, 4:1-3 en 7Q4?", *Biblica*, 53, 1972, pp. 362–367.

_____, "El cambio δ>τ en los papiros bíblicos." *Biblica*, 54, 1973.

_____, "El Ordenador, 7Q5Y Homero." *Studia Papyrologica*, 12, July–Dec., 1973, Fasc. 2.

_____, "El Ordenador, 7Q5Y Los Autores Griegos (Apolonio de Rodas, Aristoteles, Lisias)." *Studia Papyrologica*, 13, 1974, pp. 21–29.

_____, "The Identifications of 7Q." *Estratto dalla Rivista AEGYPTUS*, 56, 1976, Fasc. 1–4.

_____, "La Identificacion de Papiros Literarios (Biblicos)." *Studia Papyrologica*, 12, 1973, pp. 91–100.

_____, *Los Papiros Griegos de la Cueva 7 de Qumrân*. Madrid: Biblioteca de Antores Christianos, 1974.

_____, "¿Papiros neotestamentarios en la cueva 7 de Qumran?" *Biblica*, 53, 1972, pp. 91–100.

_____, "Sobre la Identificacion de 7Q4." *Studia Papyrologica*, 13, 1974, pp. 45–55.

_____, "Eusebio: Historia eclesiástica, Vol. 43, 7–8, 11–12 en PBerl. inv. 17076," *Studia Papyrologica*, 14, 1975, pp. 103–108.

_____, "Théocrite I 31–35, 73–78 (P. Verl. inv. 17073)." Extrait de la *Chronique d'Ègypte*, 50, 1975, pp. 192–194.

_____, "Tres probables papiros neotestamentarios en la cueva 7 de Qumrân." *Studia Papyrologica*, 11, 1972, pp. 83–89.

_____, "Notas y commentarios, ¿El texto de 7Q5 es Tuc. 1 41,2?" *Studia Papyrologica*, 13, July–Dec., 1974, p 125.

_____, "Notas y commentarios, 7Q5: Nuevas consideraciones." *Studia Papyrologica*, 16, Jan.–June 1977, pp. 41–47.

_____, "Notas sobre 7Q tomadas en el—Rockefeller Museum—de Jerusalém." *Biblica*, 53, 1972, pp. 517–533.

Orchard, B. "A Fragment of St. Mark's Gospel Dating from before A.D. 50?" *Biblical Apostolate*, Rome, 6, 1972, pp. 5–6.

Parker, P. "Enthält das Papyrus fragment 5 aus der Höhle von Qumrân einen Markustext?" *Erbe und Auftrag*, 48, 1972, pp. 467–469.

Pickering, W. N. *The Identity of the New Testament Text*. Nashville, Thomas Nelson Inc., Publishers, 1977.

Hans Quecke, *Das Markusevangelium saïdisch. Text der Handschrift PPalau Rib. Inv.–Nr. 182 mit den Varianten der Handschrift M 569*, Barcelona, 1972, Papyrologica Castroctaviana 4.

_____, *Das Lukasevangelium saïdisch. Text der Handschrift PPalau Rib. Inv.–Nr. 181 mit den Varianten der Handschrift M 569*, Barcelona, 1977, Papyrologica Castroctaviana 6.

Reicke, B. "Fragments neutestamentlicher Papyri bei Qumran?" *Theologische Zeitschrift*, Basel, 28, 1972, p. 304.

Roberts, C.H. "On Some Presumed Papyrus Fragments of the New Testament from Qumran." *The Journal of Theological Studies*, 23, 1972, pp. 446–447.

Sabourin, L. "A Fragment of Mark at Qumran?" *Biblical Theology Bulletin*, Rome, 2, 1972, pp. 308–312.

Sacchi, P. "Scoperta di frammenti neotestamentari in una grotta di Qumran." *Rivista de Storia e Letteratura Religiosa*, Florence, 8, 1972, pp. 429–431.

Spottorno, M. V. "Nota sobre los papiros de la cueva 7 de Qumran." *Estudios Clasicos*, Madrid, 15, 1972, pp. 261–263.

Vardaman, J. "The Earliest Fragments of the New Testament?" *The Expository Times*, Edinburgh, 83, 1972, pp. 374–376.

Vogt, E. "Entdeckung neutestamentlicher Texte beim Toten Meer?" *Orientierung*, Zurich, 36, 1972, pp. 138–140.

White, W., Jr. "O'Callaghan's Identifications: Confirmation and Its Consequences." *The Westminster Theological Journal*, Philadelphia, 35, 1972, pp. 15–20.

_____, "Notes on the Papyrus Fragments from Cave 7 at Qumran," *The Westminster Theological Journal*, Philadelphia, 35, 1973, pp. 221–226.